CUSTOMER SERVICE

in leisure and tourism

Books are ...
the last da...

CUSTOMER SERVICE

in leisure and tourism

ADRIAN LYONS MA

PROJECT MANAGER: JOHN EDMONDS
PROJECT CONSULTANT: DEBBIE BETTERIDGE

Hodder & Stoughton

A MEMBER OF THE HODDER HEADLINE GROUP

Orders: please contact Bookpoint Ltd, 39 Milton Park, Abingdon, Oxon OX14 4TD.
Telephone: (44) 01235 400414, Fax: (44) 01235 400454. Lines are open from 9.00 - 6.00,
Monday to Saturday, with a 24 hour message answering service.
Email address: orders@bookpoint.co.uk

British Library Cataloguing in Publication Data
Customer service in leisure & tourism. – (Hodder GNVQ.
  Leisure & tourism in action)
  1. Tourist trade – Great Britain – Management. 2. Leisure
  industry – Great Britain – Management
  338.4'791'0688

ISBN 0 340 65840 1

First published 1997
Impression number 10 9 8 7 6 5 4 3 2
Year   2004 2003 2002 2001 2000 1999 1998

Typeset by Wearset, Boldon, Tyne & Wear.
Printed in Great Britain for Hodder & Stoughton Educational, a division of Hodder
Headline Plc, 338 Euston Road, London NW1 3BH by Scotprint Ltd, Musselburgh, Scotland.

Contents

Acknowledgements   vi
Assessment matrix   vii
Introduction   ix

1 *Investigating customer service*   1
   Types and components of customer service   1
   Why is customer service important?   5
   Communication   6
   Types of customers   12
   Case Study: Holiday Inn – Garden Court, Aachen, Germany   14

2 *Investigating sales and selling as part of customer service*   19
   The functions of selling   19
   Sales techniques   23
   The duties and responsibilities of sales staff   24
   Sales administration systems   27
   What makes the selling of leisure and tourism products different?   27
   Case Study: customer service in DFDS Scandinavian Seaways   28

3 *Analysing customer service quality*   36
   Assessing the quality of customer service   36
   Appraising customer service   40
   Analysing the quality of customer service   41
   Analysing the quality offered in related markets   41
   Comparing customer service   42
   Making recommendations for improvements   43

4 *Review of the Unit*   44

Glossary   48
Crossword: investigating customer service   50
Index   51

Acknowledgements

Special thanks for their help in the writing of this book to:
Laurs Aachim (Holiday Inn – Garden Court, Aachen), Patrick Libs (General Manager of the Holiday Inn, Strasbourg); Hamish Gibson, Kerry Oxley, David Warner, John Crummie (all of Scandinavian Seaways); Jane Mellor.

The publishers would like to thank the following for permission to reproduce material:

P&O Ferries (material on p. 3); Le Shuttle (material on p. 3); British Airways (Figure 1.5); Rank Leisure Ltd (Figure 1.7); Odeon Cinemas (material on p. 5); Forte (Figures 2.2 and 3.4); IPC (Magazines Holiday Survey 1994, Figure 2.6); McDonald's (Figure 3.1); Scandinavian Seaways; Holiday Inn – Garden Court, Aachen.

Assessment Matrix

The tasks contained in this booklet will generate the Evidence Indicators of each Element of Unit 6: *Developing Customer Service in leisure and tourism*, part of the Advanced GNVQ in leisure and tourism (1995 specifications). They also meet the performance criteria of the Key Skills Elements indicated below.

The term 'Key Skills' is used instead of 'Core Skills' throughout, and the Element numbers refer to 1995 specifications.

Students may provide evidence to meet grading themes through each task at both Merit and Distinction level.

Key Skills Hint boxes precede certain tasks to give help and guidance on the particular skill developed through the task.

Task	Unit 6	Application of Number	Communication	IT
			Key Skills	
Task 1	6.1		3.2 pcs 1–5	3.3 pcs 1–6
Task 2	6.1		3.4 pcs 1–4	
Task 3	6.2		3.2 pcs 1–5	3.3 pcs 1–6
Task 4	6.2		3.3 pcs 1–3	
Task 5	6.3		3.4 pcs 1 & 4	
Task 6	6.3			
Task 7 (Review of Unit)	6.4			
Task 8 (Review of Unit)	6.4		3.1 pcs 1, 2 & 5	
Task 9 (Review of Unit)	6.4		3.2 pcs 1–5	

Introduction

WHAT DO WE MEAN BY CUSTOMER SERVICE?

Customer service is quite difficult to define because what customers expect will be different in different situations. For example, if you are visiting a hamburger restaurant for a take-away meal, you will probably want your customer service to be quick and accurate. A smiling friendly assistant might be a bonus but your main concern, and the main thing that will attract you to make a return visit, is likely to be getting precisely what you asked for, served to you quickly.

On the other hand, if you are going to a restaurant for a romantic candlelit dinner, a slow service giving you time between each course may be appreciated. In such a restaurant the emphasis may be on ambience rather than efficiency.

Customer service describes all the direct and indirect contact between an organisation and its customers. This means that in the hamburger restaurant it may be obvious that the staff who take your order are engaged in customer service, but which of the following people are also involved in customer service?

- The cook who cooks the burgers
- The manager of the restaurant
- The person cleaning the floor
- The person ordering supplies
- The person at head office negotiating a contract to buy meat of an appropriate quality
- The person devising a training programme for staff

The answer is of course that they are all engaged either directly or indirectly in 'customer service', because they all have a part to play in ensuring that the customer is satisfied with the product. Note that the product is not just the food, but the speed of service, cleanliness of the environment and friendliness of the staff.

I recently visited a café in Germany where the coffee and cakes were delicious – however, my wife wanted a cup of tea and unfortunately many German cafés and restaurants do not know how to make a decent cup of tea. There are usually two problems: the actual tea bag is often of a very good quality, being a specific variety such as Ceylon, Assam or Darjeeling, but the water is rarely boiling and, rather than fresh milk, condensed milk is offered; this second problem can often be overcome by asking for fresh milk: 'Darf ich frische Milch bitte haben?' ('May I have fresh milk please?'). After asking for tea, I asked for the fresh milk and our waitress then asked if we wanted it hot or cold. This question caught me out, and thinking that she was referring to the tea, I answered 'hot'. She went away, and my wife pointed out that the waitress was referring to the milk rather than the tea, so I went to the counter and told the waitress that I was sorry and that I had meant cold milk.

After a couple of minutes a tray came with our gorgeous cakes, a cup of coffee that I had ordered and a glass of cold milk. The customer service had so far included good food and quick service, but that was about to be ruined. I said that I was sorry but I had meant for the milk to be in the tea; I started to explain that my German was not so good because I am British, but before I had a chance to continue, the waitress started shouting at me using a string of colloquial insults that I had difficulty in translating. The milk quickly disappeared and a cup of tea (with condensed milk) was brought, accompanied by more aggressive language. As we quietly drank our drinks and ate our cake, we saw our waitress recounting the tale of these troublesome foreigners to her colleagues. Our exposure to that organisation's customer service makes it unlikely that we will return to that café.

Investigating customer service

Key Aims

This section will enable you to:

- explain just what goes to make up good customer service
- explain why customer service is important
- explain why effective communication is important
- describe different types of customer service
- carry out an investigation into a leisure or tourism organisation

TYPES AND COMPONENTS OF CUSTOMER SERVICE

This is the slogan of Laurs Aachim, sales manager at the Holiday Inn-Garden Court in Aachen. What do you think he means?

In any leisure and tourism organisation some people are going to be engaged in direct and regular customer contact; they are likely to be receptionists, waiters and waitresses, and can all be described as **front of house** (see Figure 1.1).

Other people may only occasionally have contact with customers – in a hotel this might, for example, include cleaning staff. These people can be called 'backroom staff' (they have indirect contact with customers, or occasional direct contact). Others may be 'support staff', and although they may very rarely come into contact with customers, their role in 'customer service' is still vital in giving front of house and backroom staff the support that they need in providing customers with a good service.

It is important to note that in any leisure

FIGURE 1.1 *Aachen Holiday Inn Garden Court Reception*

and tourism organisation, every staff member is engaged in customer care. Customer care simply means looking after customers. Anyone who fails to look after customers with the view that it is not their job, lets down all their colleagues.

Caring for customers

To care for your customers, you must care about their individual needs and requirements. For example, in a fast food restaurant a customer may order a hamburger but say that she does not like relish. There are three possible responses.

1 Say: 'I am very sorry madam, but the burgers come with relish already on.'
2 Say: 'Okay madam, I will see what I can do' and then give the customer a standard burger with relish.
3 Say: 'No problem madam. It'll take just another couple of minutes but I'll make sure that you get a plain burger', and then make sure that she does get a plain burger.

It is only the third option that shows customer care. However, really excellent customer service goes further than merely satisfying customers; it is concerned with exceeding their expectations. An example might be in an art gallery where no photography is allowed: a customer wants a picture of a particular painting, but the postcards you are selling in the gift shop of that particular painting have temporarily run out. You can explain this to the customer, but the caring thing to do would be to take the customer's name and address and agree to send on a postcard when new stocks arrive.

Meeting customer needs

In leisure and tourism, customers will usually have several needs, some of which may conflict with one another; for example, a couple may want to travel from Bristol to London to see a show. They may want to travel both quickly, comfortably and cheaply. The problem is that it would be cheaper for the couple to make a car journey than to travel by rail, although the train is much faster. Another consideration is that in the car you can spread out and listen to the radio or tapes, while in a train you are likely to be in a crowded carriage listening to other people's tapes. A way to avoid this discomfort is to pay extra for first class travel but this makes the trip even more expensive. Sometimes in leisure and tourism it may be necessary to help a customer to prioritise their needs to find the best fit in the services that are available.

In order to meet customer needs it is necessary to be able to identify them. This skill will develop with experience, but even from the beginning of a career in this area it is possible to start developing this skill by thinking about the customer. For example, a customer may visit a travel agent – he may be 28, but if he is taking his wife and two young children on holiday he may not want you to suggest that he goes on a Club 18–30 package.

Examine the following two texts taken from the first page of the brochure for the P&O Ferries and the Channel Tunnel. Although each is aimed at customers wishing to cross the channel with their cars, they emphasise very different customers needs.

---

1 Drive on. Unwind. Relax. This is the way to start your continental holiday. Come with us and find out why it's so much nicer to travel P&O European Ferries. Millions of people do every year and yet our modern, purpose-built Superferries and Cruiseferries always remain bright and spacious. Why? Because we know you like it that way. And the very name P&O has come to mean style, luxury and impeccable service at sea.

Source: P&O Ferries brochure

2 Le Shuttle is smooth. Le Shuttle is the direct route to France – for everyone travelling by car.

And best of all, Le Shuttle is the easiest way to travel. Buy your ticket in advance, through your local travel agent or direct by phone on 0990 35 35 35. Or pay on arrival and drive straight onto Le Shuttle.

Source: Le Shuttle brochure, 1996

Customer satisfaction

DFDS Scandinavian Seaways Customer Service & Care Task Team Mission Statement
To empower Scandinavian Seaways' managers and staff with the skills, knowledge and responsibility that will enable them to deliver a level of service to both delight and surprise our customers, and instil a feeling of pride to be working for the most professional and service minded carrier and tour operator to Scandinavia and Northern Europe.

Source: DFDS Scandinavian Seaways

Customer service is all about ensuring that the customer is completely satisfied. Satisfied customers will in turn lead to well-motivated staff. In a work situation there are few things more stressful than being confronted with many dissatisfied customers, whereas staff who treat customers with care and respect will be appreciated by the customer, and will in turn deliver a good service to the next customer. The effect is a circular one (see Figure 1.2).

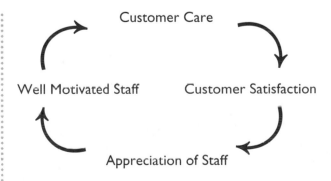

FIGURE 1.2 *The customer service cycle*

Meeting customer expectations

Expectations are not the same as needs: they can be based on advertising, reputation, previous experience, or the word of others. In fact, in leisure and tourism the recommendation of friends and colleagues often plays a very important role in choices that are made – for example, 'That film was brilliant' or 'That new restaurant was great. The food is delicious'.

The problem with these recommendations is that the customer's taste in films or food may be very different to that of the person making the recommendation. You may be unable to meet the customer's expectations and it may be beyond your ability to do so. However, if a customer is led to expect that he or she can turn up at the Channel Tunnel and 'drive straight onto Le Shuttle', but then actually has to wait 90 minutes, and is then led to believe that 'Once on board, in 35 minutes you arrive in Calais' whereas the journey from station to station lasts an hour, then the organisation has clearly failed to meet customer expectations.

Maintaining security and safety

Safety and security of customers must always take priority over every other need and expectation. If a hotel has a rule that children under 12 may not use the swimming pool without being accompanied by an adult, then you must refuse to allow the 10-year-old child into the pool, no matter how much that upsets the parents. It is helpful, and avoids confrontations, if safety rules are set out very clearly in written form.

Staff must be given adequate training in how to deal with any situation where they may be responsible for the safety of the public – for example, on car ferries all the crew must be trained in emergency procedures for evacuations; less dramatically, any staff who process or serve food should have passed the Royal Society of Health Essential Food Hygiene course (see Figure 1.3).

Leisure and tourism organisations should have clear procedures for dealing with the following situations.

- Fire
- Bomb threats
- Medical emergencies
- Visits by VIPs (Very Important People)

They should have policies that cover the following:

- Ensuring that the buildings and equipment used are safe
- Ensuring that food that is served is stored and prepared safely to avoid food poisoning
- Ensuring that anything that could present a danger (such as cleaning chemicals, or chlorine from a swimming pool) is stored and used properly. (The day before the 1996 European Cup football final, the team from the Czech Republic had to be evacuated from their hotel because of an escape of chlorine from the swimming pool!)

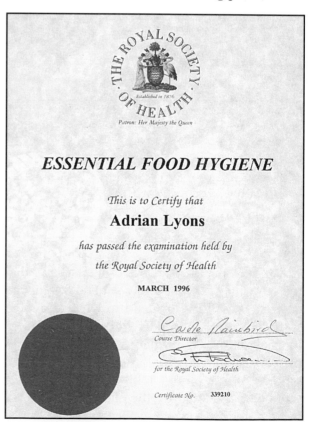

FIGURE 1.3 *Royal Society of Health Essential Food Hygiene Certificate*

- Ensuring that the behaviour of some customers does not present a hazard or a disturbance to others.

WHY IS CUSTOMER SERVICE IMPORTANT?

Odeon Cinemas answer this question in the preamble to their customer care instructions to cinema managers.

We are committed to providing the highest standard of service to our customers each and every day. We welcome each and every customer (and any complaints they may have). Our purpose is to entertain each of our customers and to ensure that they enjoy being in our cinemas.

Your commitment to your customers will impact on your business. It will ensure customer loyalty and repeat business.

Where you are in competition with other leisure facilities or other cinemas, the service you offer your customers can be the deciding factor in a customer choosing where to spend his/her money. You can make sure it is at your cinema.

Please remember that the ultimate objective of any customer interaction is to encourage repeat business.

Source: Odeon Cinemas

Ron Zemke (author of *The Service Edge*) speaking on the BBC's 'Business Matters' in 1991, argued that providing your customers with a quality service is important for the following reasons.

1 *Service is a distinguisher.* This means that where there are many businesses competing by providing a similar product, it is difficult for customers to choose who to buy that product from. You might be able to sell your product more cheaply than your competitors (thereby distinguishing it from the competition) – however, if you can afford to cut your prices it is likely that the competition would cut their prices as well. You therefore need to find some other way of attracting customers. In the high street, people continue to shop at Marks & Spencer for food although food products are available for a cheaper price in other stores; people return there because of its unrivalled reputation for quality. In leisure and tourism, the quality of the product can usually be seen in the customer service that is offered. Therefore, if you cannot distinguish your product from the competition by price, you need to do so through a good reputation for service.

For example, the Steigenberger Reservation Service is a grouping of three hotel chains with three hundred hotels all around the world. Their directory says:

'As individual as each of our valued guests, every SRS Hotel is an original. Each with its own history, charm and personality, uniquely constructed and independently managed.

Unique and yet similar. Whether visiting an exotic resort location or a vibrant city hotel, our quality grading is your guarantee that similar comfort levels and service standards can be enjoyed at the hotels in each category. So, please make your selection from any of the SRS Hotels in the "SRS Deluxe Collection", "SRS First Class Collection" or "SRS Comfort Selection" (see Figure 1.4).'

British Airways clearly sees customer service as vital to their image, as can be seen in this advert for cabin crew (see Figure 1.5).

2 *Service is a value adder.* A product has value added, when it is made more useful to the consumer, for example, one reason that tea bags are more expensive than loose leaf tea is that the tea bag is more convenient to use, therefore people are prepared to pay

The SRS Hotel Classifications

Deluxe Collection
- Noble Lodging
- Refined Elegance
- Exclusive Ambiance
- Luxurious Comfort
- Peerless Service

First Class Collection
- Superior Lodging
- Sophisticated Elegance
- Fine Ambiance
- First-Rate Comfort
- Excellent Service

Comfort Collection
- Commodious Lodging
- Natural Elegance
- Casual Ambiance
- Ample Comfort
- Attractive Price

FIGURE 1.4 *The SRS Hotel Classifications*

extra. The product has been augmented or added to. In a similar way people will be prepared to pay more if they can be assured of consistently good service.

Ron Zemke suggested that the benefits of quality service to businesses include increasing their market share (the proportion of all sales by all businesses of that product) three times faster than businesses that lack a reputation for quality service. They are also able to charge more for their products, and the business will grow in size twice as fast as others.

COMMUNICATION

Communication is vital in giving customers and potential customers an impression of your business. All staff must be aware of the importance of good communication with customers, as all employees of an organisation will be seen as part of that business by the customer. Customers do not judge an organisation by the reception desk alone – communication is about receiving as well as giving information.

The way in which you communicate with customers will be influenced by the situation. You may be:

- Communicating with individuals
- Communicating with groups
- Attempting to make a good first impression
- Attempting to present a good personal image
- Speaking on the telephone
- Having a face-to-face discussion
- Communicating in writing
- Giving information verbally
- Giving information in a non-verbal form (perhaps pointing to somewhere on a map)

Communicating with individuals

Employees such as receptionists, ushers, waiters, and bar staff can be described as 'the front line'. For these people body language is particularly important when dealing with customers.

Eye contact. Look at the person to whom you are speaking – by 'catching their eye' you hold their attention and make them feel included in what you are saying.

Gestures. Some gestures can be very distracting. Although pointing to something can be a useful way of bringing the customer's attention to an object or a direction, scratching your head while talking can be offputting.

Cabin Crew

Heathrow & Gatwick

When it comes to delivering the very best in customer service, British Airways Cabin Crew stand apart. They have the blend of skills and experience to understand and respond to customer needs and, equally importantly, they have the freedom to take those spontaneous decisions that create a special in-flight atmosphere.

Our approach is challenging the traditional view of the cabin crew role. Those who join us can look forward to using **their initiative** and people skills to the full, doing that **extra** something that makes the difference. It could be **as simple as** helping to comfort a "first time flyer" or talking to a customer in their own language... whatever it is, it demonstrates our fundamental belief that every one of the 35 million people who fly with us each year deserves individual attention — a service that goes above and beyond their expectations.

As our global network grows, we are looking for more people who can provide the essential personal touch. You must have the right to live and work in the UK indefinitely, be aged 20–49 or above, standing 5'2" - 6'2" with weight in proportion and conversational abilities in at least one of the following second languages:

FRENCH, GERMAN, ITALIAN, SPANISH, PORTUGUESE, GREEK, DUTCH, RUSSIAN, TURKISH, HEBREW, ARABIC, JAPANESE, MANDARIN, CANTONESE, THAI, KOREAN, URDU, HINDI, GUJARATI, PUNJABI, SWAHILI, ANY SCANDINAVIAN LANGUAGE, ANY EASTERN EUROPEAN LANGUAGE AND EXISTING CERTIFICATE HOLDERS OF SIGN LANGUAGE.

If you have the skills and vision to communicate with our customers and would like to know more, please telephone Pat Cook on **0181 940 5656**, Monday to Friday between 9am - 6pm.

BRITISH AIRWAYS
The world's favourite airline

FIGURE 1.5 *Advert for British Airways*

Source: The Guardian, 29 June, 1996

Give direct answers. When a customer asks a question, do your best to give a direct answer, and if you don't know, be honest.

When possible, address the individual by name to show that you value them as individuals.

Deal with one customer at a time and avoid distractions.

Communicating with groups

In many leisure and tourism situations, providing customer service involves communicating with groups; one of the most obvious of which is, perhaps, leading a group of tourists on a tour.

When communicating with a group:

- Gather everyone in closely and ensure that everyone can see and hear you

- Keep what you are saying brief and to the point – avoid digressions
- Check that everyone has understood your point before moving on (you may do this through questioning)
- Offer the opportunity for individuals to speak to you afterwards for further information

Making a good first impression

You only have one chance to make a good first impression. Remember that a customer will usually form an impression of you and your organisation within 30 seconds – it may be possible to change that impression but it will take a lot of time and effort. Get it right first time!

Personal image

The first impression that customers get of an organisation will often depend on the image of the staff and the first thing that will be noticed is your appearance, followed by your attitude to the customer and general behaviour before (finally) your skills and efficiency at dealing with the customer's needs. You might be very skilful and efficient in delivering customer service, but if your appearance creates a casual image or you are impolite to the customer, a very poor image of the organisation will be formed.

Many leisure and tourism organisations provide their staff with uniforms. There are several customer service advantages in this (see Figure 1.6).

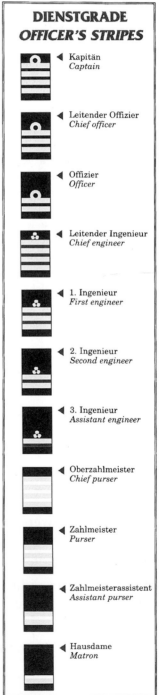

FIGURE 1.6
Scandinavian Seaways personnel are always easily identified in their uniform

- A professional corporate image is presented
- Staff can be easily recognised as part of the organisation
- Staff can be easily found by customers
- It gives the wearers a sense of belonging to a team

Speaking on the telephone

In over 95 per cent of businesses, contact with the customer will at some stage be by telephone. There are some basic rules to good customer service when being contacted by telephone:

- Answer the phone before it has rung four times
- Greet the customer and give the name of your business very clearly. Giving your own first name helps to make the reception more friendly, but at a particular level of seniority giving your business name may be more appropriate to denote that the call is being taken seriously
- Whenever a customer has had to wait (if a large number of calls are being dealt with) always apologise for the delay
- In the following extract you will see the advice to 'smile' on the telephone. This may seem silly but the expression on your face does have an impact on your voice

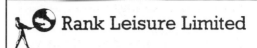 **Rank Leisure Limited**

"Another satisfied customer!"

The Guide To Good Customer Relations

SATISFACTION — THE WORD FOR SUCCESS

S stand before a mirror and examine what others will see:-
Hair.   Clean and tidy, brushed back from the face.
Dress. Simple, neat and clean -- not flash!
Hands. Clean, free of stains, no nail-biting or chipped and cracked nail varnish.

A ttention must be paid to your personal hygiene. People remember bad things and you have only one chance to create a good first impression.

T he area where you work is important. Keep it clean, tidy and free of personal property. Do not use it as a private leisure centre, no drinks, eats, chats or smoking.

I n the first few minutes of taking over, ensure you know "what's been going on" and any outstanding business. Never hand over or take over half way through a guest's reception.

S miling, even on the telephone, softens your tone of voice. You cannot sound gruff with a smile on your face — try it for yourself!

F acial expressions tell a tale. They indicate the other person's feelings. Your mouth can indicate friendliness as easily as boredom.

A ttend to guests as soon as they approach you. If you are busy or on the phone, excuse yourself and inform them that you will attend to them as soon as possible.

C omplaints can be handled easily with a simple system: Listen to what they have to say but never take it personally.
Sympathise with them, and try to mean it!

Do not try to justify what has happened, they do not want to know your problems!
Ask questions and get the facts.
Agree with them a course of action, stick to it. Follow up what you have agreed on. Check it out.

Thank them for bringing the matter to your attention. A "please" and "thank you" never go amiss, neither does a "Good morning Sir or Madam", "Can I be of assistance?

Impress upon them your awareness of their importance. People like to feel important. It is part of the service they are paying for.

Only when you are sure of an answer will you be able to deal with enquiries, so never try to bluff your way through — it just will not work. If in doubt ask your superiors, and let the guests know what you are doing.

Never forget that you are there to please, so please remember:–
Posture.   How you stand shows how you feel.
Look and listen. Pay attention to the guest.
Expression.   Your face tells it all — smile!
Appearance.   Neat in dress, neat in mind!
Speech.   Keep your tone friendly and speak clearly.
Eagerness.   Your desire to help others should be your second nature — let it show.

REMEMBER The customer is your boss, he's the one paying your wages!

FIGURE 1.7 *Another satisfied customer*

Source: Rank Leisure Limited.

In Figure 1.7, note how much customer satisfaction is down to communication.

Face-to-face meetings with customers

If you put into practice what has been covered so far, then face-to-face communication has advantages over other forms – you can smile, use eye contact and positive (but not distracting) gestures to make customers feel welcome.

Written communication

There are many forms of written communication between leisure and tourism organisations and their customers such as:

Advertisements
Price lists
Bills
Programmes
Brochures
Signs
Email
Tickets
Faxes
Timetables
Leaflets
World wide web pages
Letters

Great care needs to be taken in the preparation of written material as the customer has time to pick up on small errors. Written communication should always be produced on a computer, a spell-check should always be employed and in these days of Information Technology there is absolutely no excuse for poor presentation – even desk-top publishing packages are now quite inexpensive.

However, literacy cannot be replaced by IT skills. There are standard ways for setting out letters – always use the client's name and finish the letter 'Yours sincerely' – and when passing on messages to clients, a word processed or typed memo is better than a handwritten note.

One of the few times when handwriting can reasonably be substituted for IT is in putting together a menu, when the choice is limited and you wish to convey a personal touch; under these circumstances, a person with good calligraphy skills can handwrite the menu. *However even when the personal touch is desired, some fonts (such as 'script') are more effective than unclear handwriting.*

Menus should always include the price and bills should be itemised so that the customer can check that the correct price has been charged; the price of any service should be clearly visible before the customer orders, so that it is quite clear what the customer will be expected to pay.

Verbal communication

When speaking to customers, you must always be polite, friendly, cheerful and clear. The most important thing is never to allow your voice to show agitation even when a customer is being particularly difficult.

Non-verbal communication

There are many ways in which messages can be given to customers without the need for words: you must give the customer your undivided attention and smiling is important as it makes hostility towards you difficult (however, make sure people don't think you are laughing at them).

Even when speaking on the telephone it is important to smile as this will subconsciously mean that you maintain a friendly manner. When speaking to customers some gestures (such as pointing the way) may be helpful but others (such as touching your face) are off-putting.

---

*An example of positive communication
Reception at the Holiday Inn – Strasbourg, France*

Upon arrival after a tiring journey, a smiling receptionist greets you with the word 'Bonsoir'. According to the reply she knows whether to speak French, English or German. She asks 'How may I help you'. The customers are asked to complete a short registration card with name, address and credit card details. While one customer does this, the receptionist asks the accompanying customer if they had a pleasant journey, and if there is anything that they would particularly like to do whilst in Strasbourg. The receptionist helpfully suggests that the old town is particularly attractive in the evening when there is a light display and shows the customers on a large clear map how to get to the City centre, giving them the map to keep. Then the customers are asked if they will have time to go further afield and, as the answer is positive, suggestions for a day trip are made accompanied by map and leaflet. Finally, she asks if there is anything else that she can help with, and when the answer is no, she wishes the customers a pleasant stay – smiling throughout.

Feedback loops

Whilst communication with customers is vital to an organisation, so too is communication between staff. A feedback loop enables feedback from staff or customers to be passed on to the relevant people – where a formal feedback loop does not exist, the following situation may occur.

A customer in a hotel phones reception to complain that the television in his room is not working. The receptionist replies that she will ask the porter to attend to it. The receptionist then deals with another customer waiting at reception, while looking at her watch because her shift is due to finish in two minutes. The television is forgotten about as the receptionist finishes dealing with the customer at reception and leaves for the night.

The next morning the customer with the faulty television checks out, not mentioning the problem but making a mental note to never return to that hotel. Later that day a new customer checks into the room with the faulty television.

How could the above situation have been better handled?

If a feedback loop had been in operation the complaint could have been dealt with as follows:

1 Customer complains to receptionist
2 Receptionist records complaint in a log and passes the details to the duty manager
3 Manager contacts the night porter and directs him to the appropriate room
4 Night porter apologises for the problem
5 Checks that the TV cannot be made to work
6 Takes faulty TV away and immediately brings spare TV
7 Porter checks that TV works
8 Porter reports to the duty manager that the customer now has a working TV and is satisfied
9 Duty manager leaves a message for the duty manager of the next shift to speak to the customer personally in the morning to apologise for the problem.

The importance of effective communication

We have now looked at a range of communication methods and it is likely that several of these forms of communication will be used together in order to be effective. Effective communication leads to:

• Customer satisfaction
• Staff satisfaction
• Increased organisational efficiency
• Increased organisational effectiveness

To be efficient, an organisation must use its resources in the best way possible; for example, having unoccupied rooms in a hotel is inefficient, as the hotel has resources (rooms) that are not being used and therefore are not bringing in income.

To be effective, an organisation must be successful in achieving its aims as expressed in its mission statement. For example, the Holiday Inn hotel group has introduced a computerised booking system called 'sales master'. As a result, booking for Holiday Inn hotels is made easier as hotels are able to judge when they are likely to be full and when they are likely to have spare capacity, and should therefore make available special offers. This increases efficiency which will in turn increase effectiveness because the organisation's aim of increasing the number of guests staying at Holiday Inn and delivering good customer service is achieved.

TYPES OF CUSTOMERS

The leisure and tourism industry has a number of different types of customers with differing needs and interests.

Internal customers

Internal customers are fellow employees of an organisation (i.e. colleagues, management and staff teams), or suppliers from outside the organisation who contribute towards the service that is provided. For example, Scandinavian Seaways' UK sales operation relies on the company's ships to provide the service and the ships rely on the sales operation to provide the customers – the sales operation and the ships are therefore internal customers of each other.

External customers

The hotel market caters to a wide range of different customers of different ages, ranging from a family with little money to spend on their annual holiday, to the business traveller who will be staying just one night, and to high expense account executives who are willing to pay for very good service. In the past these 'market segments' would have stayed in very different hotels to one another, but nowadays they are likely to use the same hotels. This is because during the early 1990s, people travelling on business found that their budgets for overnight accommodation were reduced; faced with smaller revenues from business customers, hotels that had been attracting mainly business customers now seek to attract families, by offering relatively cheap offers at times when the business customers tend to be at home. At the Forte Posthouse chain of hotels, an overnight stay on any night from Monday to Thursday costs £59 per room (excluding breakfast). However, at the weekend when the business customers have gone home, you can get a two night break (which must include a Saturday night) at the Colchester Post House for £78 each including dinner and breakfast.

A common way of breaking down customers into groups so that their particular needs may be taken into account is as follows:

- Age group
- Cultural background
- Customers with specific needs
- Individuals
- Groups

Age groups

This is a useful generalisation for targeting your service at groups of customers. Your service may be aimed at children, but are they babies, toddlers, older children or teenagers? They all have very different needs.

If you are dealing with adults, are they young adults, middle-aged or senior citizens?

Of course family groups are likely to include any, or all, of the above as well as adults with babies or young children, adults with teenage children, children with senior citizen grandparents or middle-aged adults with senior citizen parents (these are all common combinations).

Never take it for granted that your customers' needs are going to fit your expectation of the needs of that age group.

Cultural background

Respecting the cultural traditions of customers is very important if you are to avoid customer dissatisfaction or avoid giving offence. For example the Salvation Army is a teetotal organisation, therefore if your confer-

ence centre is hosting a big Salvation Army meeting it would be wise to stock the bar with a range of soft drinks rather than alcoholic beverages (the same is true of Muslims and you would of course avoid serving pork at a Jewish celebration meal). However, taking account of cultural background can be more positive than just avoiding things – the provision of separate women-only swimming sessions may be influenced by the fact that Islam forbids social contact between men and women in public, but it may also prove very popular with non-Muslim women as well.

In many countries it is common to be offered a guided tour of a tourist attraction with a commentary in English or several other languages. In many European countries it is common to find people employed in leisure and tourism who are able to speak fluent English, while in Britain it is rare to find somebody able to communicate in a foreign language. So, for example the guides that give conducted tours of the Hellbrunn Palace outside Salzburg, Austria take mixed nationality groups around, giving explanations and answering questions in equally fluent German, English, French and Italian.

Specific needs

Customers may have specific special needs because of problems with:

- Sight
- Hearing
- Mobility
- Literacy and numeracy
- Language
- Diet

It is important that people with specific needs should not feel patronised – remember that people are often not disabled so much by their impairment as by the environment. If somebody in a wheelchair needs help they will usually ask for it so do not assume that the customer is helpless, but always give any assistance that is requested by the customer. Never ignore the customer with specific needs by talking only to their partner. Treat the customer with the same respect and courtesy as anyone else.

Individuals

In some situations people using leisure and tourism as individuals have special needs just because they are individuals. For example, some hotels make special arrangements for women staying alone, by offering women customers the chance to partner up with another woman staying on her own at dinner, to avoid the unwelcome attention of male customers.

In many hotels, VIPs are not necessarily the rich and the famous but may be frequent visitors to the hotel or representatives of businesses who bring a lot of custom to the hotel, and who therefore need to be treated with special care. The Holiday Inn at Strasbourg's policy for dealing with their VIPs is to give them special treatment by:

- Training the hotel staff to recognise and acknowledge them
- Ensuring they receive a special welcome
- Arranging for a bottle of Alsace (local) wine and a welcome letter from the manager to be placed in their room
- Arranging for a local gift to be left in their room

Groups

Groups are usually welcome in leisure and tourism organisations as they bring in a lot of customers and, in a hotel, can fill a lot of rooms or many tables in a restaurant. For this reason organisations are usually pleased to welcome groups and are willing to offer large discounts to attract them. However, the unexpected arrival of a coach-load of customers at 4 am at a motorway service station, all wanting a big breakfast, can stretch the ability to offer good customer service. In such circumstances the same rules should be followed as in other situations, but you should also apologise and explain that there may be some delay.

CASE STUDY: HOLIDAY INN — GARDEN COURT, AACHEN, GERMANY

The world-wide Holiday Inn organisation is actually a British owned company based in Atlanta, USA. It either operates itself or **franchises** more than 1,900 hotels (with 355,000 bedrooms) in more than 60 countries around the world. Holiday Inn claims to be the world's single largest hotel **brand**.

When the first Holiday Inn hotel was opened in Memphis, USA in 1952, its proprietor – Kemmons Wilson – introduced a new standard. The first hotel allowed children to stay free, and offered a swimming pool, air-conditioning and restaurant, together with telephones and large parking space. All of these were unusual at the time. However, it was the commitment to offer 'customers consistently high standards in middle-market lodging, the **segment of the market** where 65% of travellers chose to stay' that became Holiday Inn's **unique selling point**. Wilson's attention to quality control and customer service would eventually make Holiday Inn the best known hotel brand in the world. (See Holiday Inn World Wide Web home pages – http://www.holiday-inn.com.)

Wilson had clearly hit on an idea for which there was great demand, and he soon realised that he did not have to own all of the hotels to make money from his concept of customer service. He offered other companies the opportunity to use his brand name 'Holiday Inn'. The hotels using this name received the benefit of people booking with them because of the quality and customer service they associated with Holiday Inn. In return each hotel buying the right to use the name 'Holiday Inn' has to agree to provide the same standards as the Holiday Inn company's own 90 hotels. One hotel using the name 'Holiday Inn' but failing to maintain the expected standards, would dent the reputation of all 1,900 hotels world-wide.

As the number of Holiday Inn hotels grew rapidly during the 1980s, it was decided to denote the facilities one could expect, by adding to the brand name. The traditional Holiday Inn still exists, but there is 'Holiday Inn – Crowne Plaza' catering for the top end of the travel market, while 'Holiday Inn – Garden Court' generally has less facilities and is rather cheaper. However, they all seek to offer the same guarantee of quality and customer service, as well as good value for money.

The Holiday Inn – Garden Court at Aachen in Germany is a franchised hotel, owned and managed by Queens Gruppe Deutschland, a **subsidiary** company of the British hotel group, Moat House. Aachen is situated in the far West of Germany, right on the border of both the Netherlands and Belgium. It has a population of around 245,000 and is an important commercial centre for the surrounding region. Its main tourist attractions are the Cathedral (the centre of which was built around the year 800 as the church attached to the palace of the most famous Frankish king, Charlemagne, who used Aachen as his capital) and the City Hall which now occupies the other end of what was Charlemagne's royal palace. There are therefore many good historical reasons for Aachen being a centre of leisure and tourism, but there is also a contemporary reason – Aachen is the most westerly site for a German Christmas market which runs each year from the last week in November up until December 22nd (see Figure 1.8).

The problem for Laurs Aachim (sales manager of Aachen's Holiday Inn – Garden Court) is that from Monday night until Friday breakfast 95 per cent of the customers are business customers, while only 5 per cent are staying for leisure. From Friday evening until Monday breakfast the situation is reversed, with 95 per cent of customers staying for leisure (or for tourism which may not be the same thing at all), and 5 per cent staying on business.

The Holiday Inn – Garden Court is not the only hotel offering good quality accommodation in Aachen, and with good road and rail communications, the numbers of visitors staying overnight in Aachen is limited. For example, by motorway the large city of Cologne is 69 kms away which takes just 40 minutes, and the German seat of Government at Bonn is just 47 kms away, or around 45 minutes drive. Outside of Germany, the EU capital in Brussels is only 1 hour and 20 minutes away at 146 kms. Faced with this limited market, the Holiday Inn has to provide consistently good service as an unsatisfactory visit will probably lead the customer to choose an alternative hotel on subsequent visits to the town, and advising colleagues to do the same.

However, Laurs decided that being 'just as good' as the competition was not good enough. The hotel needed a **unique selling point**, but the scope for extra facilities was

FIGURE 1.8 *Aachen's Christmas Market*

limited. The hotel does not have a swimming pool but hotel pools are expensive to build and run. They use a lot of water, chemicals, energy for heating and staff time as they need to be supervised. No extra income is generated unless there is demand from the local population to pay to use the pool. This would not be the case in Aachen as there is a leisure club nearby.

For relatively little extra money, Laurs has marketed the hotel as 'the friendliest hotel in Aachen'. All staff are expected to be polite and friendly – when walking along the corridor cleaning staff will greet you with a cheery 'Guten Morgen'. This costs nothing of course, but staff need to be motivated to do it. Regular staff meetings remind all the staff that their jobs depend on the hotel attracting customers. This takes place in regular departmental meetings, but every three months there is an information meeting for all staff when they are informed of the activities of the sales office and encouraged to think of themselves as each being an integral part of the customer service provision of the hotel. Additionally, in each bedroom there are little 'friendly' touches such as the suggestion to phone home (see Figure 1.9).

In 1995, the Holiday Inn – Garden Court at Aachen received 22,000 guests of which only 2,500 were booked through Holiday Inn central reservations. This centrally-booked number has increased from 1,750 in 1994 due to greater use of information technology. However, it seems that despite the worldwide **brand recognition** of Holiday Inn, it is the hotel itself that attracts guests. Information on the number of people who return to the hotel for a second visit is not recorded, but at the time of writing there were six people who stayed in the hotel for several days each week.

Of course things can still go wrong and it is important to try to limit the damage when breakdowns in customer service occur. If a customer is dissatisfied, the principle must be not to just satisfy the customer, but to give them more than they might reasonably expect. For example, a customer booked a

FIGURE 1.9 *The friendly touch*

non-smoking bedroom at Aachen Holiday Inn – Garden Court, through central reservations, for later that evening. When the customer arrived, the receptionist said that the customer was not expected; she then went to check on the computer and found that booking had come through since the last time it had been checked. However, no non-smoking rooms were available which meant that the customer had to be given an ordinary bedroom. When the customer wrote to the hotel manager to complain, the customer received a letter of apology, together with a voucher for a free two-night stay, with a complimentary dinner on the first night, for any weekend of the customer's choosing. When the customer arrived in his room for the free weekend there was a bowl of fresh fruit waiting and a very special fuss was made of the customer and his wife at dinner.

This sounds quite expensive for the hotel but at the weekend the hotel is not very busy so the room would have probably been empty anyway. The hotel calculates that the extra cost of having people occupying a room is 40 Deutschmarks (about £17) per night. The gain for the hotel is that the customer has returned several times and paid the full rate of 155 Deutschmarks (approximately £67) at the weekend, and during holiday periods or 250 Deutschmarks (approximately £109) for staying midweek.

It has already been said that Holiday Inn hotels are independently run and the reputation of all Holiday Inn hotels depends on the others. It is therefore important to maintain standards. This is done in three ways:

1 *Guest interviews.* Representatives from Holiday Inn visit each hotel and interview customers in the lobby.
2 *Quality standards check.* Several times a year representatives of Holiday Inn make a formal inspection of the hotel to check on levels of cleanliness and that the hotel is investing in new service and the upkeep of the hotel. Ten bedrooms are checked, as are the public spaces and the kitchen. Holiday Inn representatives may also stay at a hotel in the normal course of their work or leisure in which case they give the manager informal feedback.
3 *Quality Awards.* Every Holiday Inn hotel competes for a variety of awards. The Holiday Inn Quality Excellence Award was won by The Aachen Holiday Inn – Garden Court in a competition covering all aspects of operations, premises and customer

service. In Germany, out of 66 Holiday Inn hotels, Aachen was one of only six to win such an award (see Figure 1.10).

Key Skills Hint: Business report writing

This will help you to provide evidence for element 2.2 and produce written material.

A report is written for a specific purpose and is generally giving information that you have, to somebody who needs that knowledge in an easily usable form. This is often because you are advising a manager who will have to make decisions based on your advice.

A report should include the following:

1 **A title page** to give a title for your report.
2 **An abstract:** a short summary of the information, how you found it out, your conclusions and recommendations.
3 **An introduction:** this should say why the report is being presented, who asked you to do it, why the information is useful, and how you are going about gathering the information.
4 **The information you wish to give (findings):** your findings will be the information you wish to give, but will need to be based on evidence, i.e. not 'I think', but 'I have found' or 'I have discovered'.
5 **Conclusions and recommendations:** these will draw together what you have discovered, putting the main points into a sensible order. You will make your recom-

FIGURE 1.10 *Aachen Holiday Inn Quality Excellence Award*

mendations based on your judgement, using the evidence you have presented in your findings.

6 Any appendices: this is the place to include any material which is referred to in the report, but which does not really fit into your flow, for example, questionnaires or lots of statistics. You would write in the report 'see appendix 1' etc. and include your appendices at the end.

A report should be written as a series of separate short paragraphs. Number your paragraphs as in the section above or when word processing, bullet points can be used.

TASK 1

You have been commissioned to produce a booklet on 'Effective customer service in leisure and tourism'. The booklet is for use by employees new to leisure and tourism. The booklet must explain what is involved in customer service, and why it is important. You must include a section on communication and explain in your own words why this is important for:

• Customer satisfaction
• Staff satisfaction
• Increased organisational efficiency
• Increased organisational effectiveness.

The booklet must also explain the different types of customers (internal and external) that may be met in leisure and tourism. Use the information and case studies given in this section to help you.

The booklet must be word processed and you may wish to include supporting information in numerical or graphical form.

CHECKLIST OF PORTFOLIO EVIDENCE

☑ a booklet produced by IT

TASK 2

Select two leisure and tourism organisations in your local area. One must be from the leisure and recreation section such as a cinema, theatre, museum, funfair, restaurant, pub, or sports ground. The other must be from the travel and tourism industry, such as a travel company, travel agency, hotel or the local tourist office.

Write a detailed business report on the chosen organisations, covering what is involved in their customer service, and why it is important. Try to **analyse** and **evaluate** the effectiveness of the organisation's customer service, and, in particular, the effectiveness of

communication between the organisation and its customers. You may illustrate your findings by including leaflets, cards, brochures etc.

Once you have chosen the organisations (and before you begin your research) you should seek advice from your teacher or lecturer concerning the possibilities for completing this research with these organisations.

CHECKLIST OF PORTFOLIO EVIDENCE

☑ a business report

Investigating sales and selling as part of customer service

Key Aims

This section will enable you to:

- explain just what is involved in selling a leisure or tourism product and why selling is an important part of customer service
- describe some techniques involved in selling leisure or tourism products
- explain the duties of staff involved in selling and the qualities needed by those staff
- explain why it is important to have a sales administration system
- explain why selling leisure and tourism products is different from selling other products
- carry out an investigation into sales and selling in a leisure or tourism organisation

THE FUNCTIONS OF SELLING

Many jobs in leisure and tourism have selling as at least part of their role. For example you may not associate selling with being a resort representative for a package holiday company, as you would expect the customers to have bought their 'package' at the travel agency. However, the resort representative will often be expected to make a good proportion of his or her income from receiving commission for **locally** arranged excursions.

Selling does not merely involve taking the customer's money and putting it in the till. It involves:

- Providing product information

- Maintaining good relations
- Operating complaints procedures
- Resolving problems

Providing product information

Customers can only make an informed choice between products available if they have sufficient information. Remember from section 1 that although you may be delivering a satisfactory service to the customer, if it does not match customer expectations it will lead to customer dissatisfaction.

You must not allow your own tastes, preferences or opinions to restrict the choice that you give the customer. In travel agencies, customers are becoming increasingly aware that staff are sometimes rewarded for selling the holidays of one particular company. The discerning customer will sense this practice. You should not invent information in an effort to please customers – it will backfire when they discover the truth for themselves. If you are uncertain about information that is requested, offer to check the information and get back to them.

Maintaining good customer relations

The Hotel Post in the beautiful Austrian town of Millstatt sends all its summer customers a Christmas card. This is a way of maintaining good customer relations, showing the customer that they are remembered several months after their departure. It is an extension of the customer care shown during their stay (see Figure 2.1).

Remember that the maintenance of good customer relations is vital to attract repeat business.

Operating a complaints procedure

Dealing with complaints is very definitely part of selling because a badly-handled complaint will lose the organisation future business, but a well-handled complaint may make the customer more likely to return, or recommend you to others. It is one of the most difficult parts of working in any organisation as the customer may be criticising a colleague or yourself. They may be angry and shout; you must remain calm and polite in response and this can be difficult. No matter how the customer treats you, bear in mind that 'The customer is always right', even when they are obviously not!

When dealing with complaints you should follow these rules:

- Never argue with the customer
- Ignore any personal comments
- Avoid allowing the volume of your voice to rise, and keep your body language calm and polite
- Empower the customer by giving them choices such as 'I'm really very sorry sir, it shouldn't have happened. Can we offer you free tickets for another night or would you rather have your money refunded?'

As we saw on pages 16–17, the Holiday Inn – Garden Court, Aachen, sees complaints as an opportunity to improve its image, and therefore secure repeat business.

We promise that throughout your stay with us, we will endeavour to meet the high standards that you expect from Holiday Inn hotels.

However, should anything not be to your satisfaction, please do not hesitate to tell us. Just call the Duty Manager or General Manager who will make every effort to put things right, as you are not expected to pay for unsatisfactory service.

If, for any reason, the hotel staff are unable to resolve the problem to your satisfaction, please call the Guest Relations Department on one of the *toll-free* numbers on the back cover.

Source: Holdiay Inn – Garden Court, Aachen

Der Millstättersee im Winter

FIGURE 2.1 *Christmas card from Hotel Post, Millstatt*

Resolving problems

Problems are not the same thing as complaints, but in many respects they need to be handled in the same way; they are usually not the fault of your organisation but are affecting customers for whom you are responsible. Problems dealt with well can bring return business while problems dealt with badly can ensure that your organisation earns a bad reputation.

The objectives of selling

It is important to bear in mind just why selling is important. Remember the Holiday Inn – Garden Court, Aachen holds regular meetings where the staff are reminded that customer service = increased sales = paying their wages.

The objectives of selling are:

- Securing repeat business
- Increasing sales

- Achieving customer satisfaction
- Increasing profitability
- Securing a competitive advantage

These objectives are all inter-related.

Securing repeat business

According to David Clutterbuck (Chairman of The Item Group)

- It costs five times more to gain new customers than to keep existing ones
- The longer the customer is with you the more they spend each year.

Source: BBC Television

It is much easier to get customers to return (assuming they are treated well) than to attract new customers. Organisations therefore try to promote customer loyalty as with the special promotions available to holders of the Forte Gold Card illustrated in Figure 2.2.

Increasing sales

Any organisation that believes it has a worth-while product to sell will want more and more people to benefit from it.

Note that increasing sales cannot always be measured by recording more money in tills. For example, a public library is free to enter and its main service of book lending is free, but it is still a leisure and tourism organisation with an objective of increasing sales.

Achieving customer satisfaction

Remember that 'good' selling is not getting the customer to spend as much as possible. It is sending the customer away satisfied with a product that meets his or her needs so that he or she will return and buy from you in the future.

Win a free one week holiday to Le Méridien Paradise Cove, Mauritius!

AIR MAURITIUS

FORTE
Gold Card

Spend £100 with your Forte Gold Card, between 1st and 31st May this year, and complete the tie-breaker, to be entered into our amazing competition to win the trip of a lifetime to the spectacular tropical retreat of Le Méridien Paradise Cove, situated in the idyllic waters of the Indian Ocean.

you will be able to discover the Creole specialities of shark meat and grilled barracuda, in one of the hotel's first class restaurants. Whatever you enjoy on holiday, this trip "to the land of smiles" will certainly be an un-forgettable experience.

When you have spent £100 with your Forte Gold Card, just complete the tie-breaker and return this postcard to us to be entered into the competition for two free flights and five complimentary nights accommodation at Le Méridien Paradise Cove.

red into the competition,

and return this postcard (freepost). To ensure that
e entered, please make sure it is fully completed
e reverse for Terms and Conditions.)

Mr Mrs Miss Ms Other

Postcode

No. | 3 | 3 | 6 | 1 | | | | | | | | |

Please complete the following tie-breaker in no more than 20 words

Mauritius is a good holiday destination because

I confirm that I have spent £100 with my Forte Gold Card (between 1st and 31st May 1996), and I have completed the tie-breaker, and wish to be entered into the competition.

Signature   Date

FIGURE 2.2 *Forte Gold Card holder's offer*

Increasing profitability

If an organisation has more money coming in during a year than it is paying out, then it is making a profit. The money flowing into an organisation is called **revenue**, and what it pays out is its **costs** (revenue − costs = profit). Most (but by no means all) leisure and tourism organisations aim to make a profit. This is especially true in the **private sector** but it can also be true of organisations in the **public sector** such as local council-owned leisure centres.

It is important to get the balance right between trying to increase your organisation's profit, and not selling customers things that they really do not want.

Securing a competitive advantage

Holiday Inn – Garden Court has tried to give itself a competitive advantage over other hotels in the city by emphasising its friendliness.

SALES TECHNIQUES

It would be a good idea to refer back to section 1, pages 9–11 to review 'handling of complaints'. Remember that repeat business is only secured by satisfied customers who have a positive image of you and your organisation.

Preparing for the sales interview

The best way to prepare for any sales interview is to ensure that you have good knowledge of the products available. For example if you are a Lakes and Mountains resort representative based in an Austrian village such as St Wolfgang, you will be trying to sell a series of excursions by coach to places such as Salzburg, Vienna, Bertchesgaden, etc. You will need to explain to customers who have paid for a holiday in St Wolfgang exactly why they cannot afford to miss the opportunity to pay another £20 each to visit these places. You will need to be enthusiastic about them and to do this, you really need to have visited them yourself.

Approaching the customer

Generally people do not like to feel pressured into buying something and this is especially true of the leisure and tourism industry when people are often trying to relax. On the other hand people do not like to be ignored; there is therefore a delicate balance to be achieved between being available to a customer who wants to buy a product and avoiding pressure. It is usually possible to read from a customer's body language whether they require assistance, but a greeting to the customer can put the ball in their court – if you open the conversation with a friendly greeting then the customer can choose whether to continue the conversation.

Identifying customer needs

'Can I help you?' is a good way of starting a conversation to get a general outline of what the customer is after, such as a holiday to a particular destination or tickets for a particular show. However, often the customer may only have a vague idea about what their needs are. For example, a customer phoned DFDS Scandinavian Seaways knowing that he wanted to go to a conference in Sweden in October. He was to drive and to visit some people he knew en route. The sales staff were able to present him with alternatives by asking questions which identified his actual needs for travel, accommodation and price. This took time because the customer started the conversation with only a very vague view of the service he required.

Sales negotiating

At times you may not be able to sell the customer exactly what they want: this may be due to the availability of the product or the amount the customer is prepared to pay. Negotiation involves explaining that although what the customer wants cannot be provided, a slightly different alternative can. For example, you may want to book a single cabin for your Scandinavian Seaways crossing which is very expensive! The sales staff will advise you of the alternatives such as sharing a two or four berth cabin or couchette.

Overcoming objections

This does not mean encouraging customers to buy products which they don't really want, but involves providing customers with information and reassurance that their objections are unfounded.

Closing the sale

Closing the sale means getting the customer to buy the product that you are selling. Although it is your aim throughout, any attempt to rush to this point may mean that the sale is lost. Sometimes it will not be possible to close the sale immediately as when a large amount of money is involved, the customer may quite reasonably want time to think and to consider the alternatives.

Sales reporting

Sometimes a sale will be recorded quite simply by ringing up the sale on a cash register that prints a till receipt (such as in a leisure centre). In more complex organisations such as Scandinavian Seaways it is vital that the sale is recorded on the computer so that the ship does not become over-booked for a particular sailing.

Sales recording

In many leisure and tourism situations a booking is made in advance and therefore needs to be recorded. This is usually done on a booking form of some kind which needs to be designed so that it contains all the information that the operator needs, but is also clear and easy for the customer to complete (see Figure 2.3).

Time management

It is important to strike a balance between giving customers all the help that they need, while not keeping potential customers waiting a long time. This is a difficult balance which requires tact. Offering to send information or giving pre-printed information to read can be helpful.

Sales presentation

This is a meeting where information on a product is given to the customer in a planned and formal way. While you may respond to customer questions, you must try to anticipate exactly what the customer needs to know about the product, and present this information in a positive manner.

THE DUTIES AND RESPONSIBILITIES OF SALES STAFF

Customer service

Selling should be the end-result of good customer service. If you concentrate your energies on selling the product you are likely to put off the customer – if you concentrate on meeting the customer's needs and expectations a sale will naturally result.

Point of sale service

Also known as the **customer interface**, the point of sale is the place where a sale takes place. This could be in a variety of places such as: a cinema box office, a hotel reception, a golf course club house or a hamburger counter.

SCANDINAVIAN SEAWAYS

Transportation Booking Form 1996

FAX BACK: 01255 244 382 or 0191 293 6222
TELEPHONE: 0990 333 000

Or Post to: Scandinavian Seaways, Scandinavia House, Parkeston Quay, Harwich, Essex, CO12 4QG.

Scandinavian Seaways Booking number (if applicable)

Name of person making a booking

Title _____ First Name _____
Surname _____
Address _____

Postcode _____

Age _____ Tel Daytime _____ Evening _____

Other persons travelling with you. Title, First Name and Surname
1. _____ Age _____
2. _____ Age _____
3. _____ Age _____
4. _____ Age _____
5. _____ Age _____

For Groups of over 10 persons you are recommended to contact the Groups Department direct on 01255 243 243. Please note that under Swedish law we must register the age of all passengers.

Where do you wish to travel?

Please tick the appropriate box to indicate your choice of destination
ESBJERG ☐ (Depart Harwich)   GOTHENBURG ☐ (Depart Harwich or Newcastle)   HAMBURG ☐ (Depart Harwich or Newcastle)   AMSTERDAM ☐ (Depart Newcastle)

When would you like to travel ?

Please check carefully on the relevant Timetable pages when there are sailings available for your chosen route.

Please write full details of any other connecting ferry route that you would like to book including departure port, date and time, return port, date and time and cabin types required where appropriate. Use a separate sheet if required.

Departure Port _____   Outward Sailing Date _____
Return Port _____   Inward Sailing Date _____

Ship Accommodation

Please tick the appropriate box to indicate which type of cabin and number of berths you require.
No. of berths   4-BERTH ☐   3-BERTH ☐   2-BERTH ☐   SINGLE ☐
Type of cabin   OUTSIDE CABIN ☐   INSIDE CABIN ☐   COUCHETTE/ECONOMY ☐   COMMODORE ☐   COMMODORE DE LUXE ☐   WASHBASIN ONLY ☐

Type of Fare

Please indicate the type of fare you wish to use.
STANDARD SINGLE ☐   STANDARD RETURN ☐
SEAPEX RETURN ☐   ECONOMY RETURN ☐
ALL IN A CAR Weekday ☐   ALL IN A CAR Weekends ☐

Please indicate any discount that you are entitled to where applicable.
YOUTH GROUP REDUCTION (10+ persons) ☐   FAMILY SAVER (Children aged 4-15) ☐
ADULT GROUP REDUCTION (10+ persons) ☐   SENIOR VOYAGERS (over 60 years) ☐
STUDENT DISCOUNT ☐   MILITARY PERSONNEL ☐

Vehicle Details

Please tick which box best describes your vehicle and complete this section
CAR ☐   MINIBUS ☐   MOTOR CARAVAN ☐   CAR +TRAILER ☐   CAR + CARAVAN ☐   COACH ☐
SCOOTER/ MOTORCYCLE/ MOPED ☐   MOTORCYCLE WITH SIDE CAR ☐   BICYCLE ☐

Make/ Model _____   Registration No _____
Insurer _____   Date first registered _____
Total length (metres) _____   Total height (metres) _____
including caravan, trailer, tow bar etc   including luggage, aerials, caravan, trailer

Train Connections

British Rail Tickets required
From: _____ Date _____
To: _____ Date _____
NUMBER OF ADULTS ☐ NUMBER OF CHILDREN ☐
CLASS – STANDARD ☐ FIRST CLASS ☐

Insurance

Personal Travel Insurance ☐   Days _____ No of Adults _____   No of Children (2-11yrs) _____
Motor Travel Insurance ☐   Days _____ Date first registered _____   Market value of vehicle _____   Motorised Caravan ☐   Caravan or Trailer ☐
Other motor insurer _____
Vehicle in Transit Insurance ☐   Days _____ Date first registered _____   Market value of vehicle _____   Other motor insurer _____
Cancellation Only Insurance ☐
Travel Worldwide Policy   Family Cover ☐   Additional children under 18 yrs (if more than 2) ☐   Motoring cover ☐

Payment

When calculating your fare please ensure that you refer carefully to the fare tables on pages 12 to 21 with regard cabin types, vehicle fares and dates of travel.

Total Fare   £ _____
Connecting Ferry fares + £ _____
(where available)
Total Insurance premium + £ _____
British Rail Tickets + £ _____
Additional discounts = £ _____
TOTAL = £ _____

Total fares can not be guaranteed until final confirmation invoice is received.

We can accept the following cards for payment
MasterCard/Visa/Delta/Switch/Diners Club/American Express

Name on card _____
Signature _____
Card Expiry date _____
My card number is _____

Do not complete this credit/charge card section if booking with a travel agent.

Special Requests

If you have any other special requests please write details either here or on an attached sheet.

Agents Stamp

ABTA Travel Agent or Motoring Organisation

Declaration

On behalf of those named above, I agree to the terms and conditions printed on page 30. I declare that to the best of my knowledge the vehicle mentioned above is in good mechanical condition, of proprietary make, fully road worthy and serviced in accordance with the manufacturers recommendations.

Principal Signature _____   Date _____

Agency Tel: _____
Agency Ref: _____
ABTA No: _____

31

PASSENGER SHIPPING ASSOCIATION MEMBER

FIGURE 2.3 *Scandinavian Seaways Booking form*

Sales information and assistance

In order to give information and assistance you must know about the alternative products on offer, and be able to use your experience to help the customer to decide on a product that will meet their needs, expectations and budget. Completing a booking form for the customer can be helpful, but you must be confident about how to do it.

Product knowledge

Of course, no matter how familiar you are with the products that you are selling, you cannot retain all the information for which you may be asked in your memory. It is therefore important to have easy access to sources of information – it does no harm to say 'I will just check that for you' and spend a few seconds looking up a particular price on a chart to ensure accuracy. Leaving a customer for 30 minutes while you visit the reference libraries is not good customer service!

After-sales service

Scandinavian Seaways after-sales service includes the issuing of port maps, clear signposting to the terminal, and giving directions to the hotel for inclusive holidays. When prebooked tickets are sent to customers, the name of the person who assembled the pack is included, giving the customer an identifiable person who has taken personal responsibility for that pack. If anything (such as an accommodation voucher) is missing it is the responsibility of that member of staff – this has improved the quality of the after-sales service.

Payments and refunds

It is the duty of sales staff to ensure that the correct amount has been paid as possibly the worst possible impression that can be made with a customer, is to find that they have paid too much. Acceptable methods of payment should also be made clear. On a recent day visit to the Swiss city of Basle, I chose a café which displayed the MasterCard sign to buy coffee and cakes. When I came to pay with my Mastercard, they told me that the minimum amount was 20 Swiss francs and my bill had only come to 17. This was not good customer service.

Refunds are a difficult area and businesses will generally have policies about when a refund can be made. This decision will often be taken at management level, and the relevant question to be considered is 'did the customer receive the service that they had paid for?'

Promoting the organisation and related products

All staff have a duty to be positive about their employing organisation. A conversation between two employees which is negative about some aspect of the organisation and is overheard by customers or potential customers can lead to a poor public image and loss of custom. A lack of customers can put your job at risk! While many people appreciated Gerald Ratner's honesty when he told a conference that his company's products were rubbish, his business' sales plummeted and he lost his job as head of the company.

Personal qualities required by sales staff

Patrick Libs, general manager of Strasbourg Holiday Inn says that the most important personal quality of his staff is that they should always smile. He says that if they make a mistake, so long as they are always friendly it does not matter. However, we have seen that there are several additional qualities (associated with an individual's personality) for successful selling as part of customer service: enthusiasm, honesty, intelligence, initiative and (of course) friendliness.

The individual also needs knowledge about the product and the alternatives that are available within the organisation, and the rest of the industry. For example, a family arrived at Harwich intending to take a short break in Legoland in Denmark. Unfortunately they missed the ferry and there was not another for 48 hours. Scandinavian Seaways passenger manager David Warner was able to use his knowledge to offer the customers the option of travelling with an alternative shipping operator (Stena Line) from Harwich to the Hoek van Holland, and making a long drive that would get them to the same destination only a few hours late. David was also able to use his judgement as to what was the best option given the situation.

Another essential quality of staff is consistency. It's not good enough to be friendly, intelligent and enthusiastic on good days only!

SALES ADMINISTRATION SYSTEMS

A sales administration system is any method of recording that a sale has been made – increasingly this is being done on computer. However, paper is still used, particularly when taking down information from customers such as on a booking form. Sales administration systems are of value to the organisation, but also to the customer as an effective sales administration system will ensure that the customer gets exactly what was ordered.

The issuing of tickets will flow from the booking form as part of a sales administration system. Other systems might also be used as follows:

- Customer accounts
- Membership lists
- Registration (keeping a record of who has arrived)
- Order processing (passing on the required information to people who need to know e.g. reception telling hotel housekeeping staff that a room is needed)
- Credit clearance (checking that a customer has sufficient credit available on the card to pay the bill)

WHAT MAKES THE SELLING OF LEISURE AND TOURISM PRODUCTS DIFFERENT?

Intangible products

Scandinavian Seaways' Hamish Gibson (customer sales and service manager) used a nice expression to sum up what makes the selling of leisure and tourism different: he said that you are asking people to part with a lot of money to 'buy a dream'. The product is intangible – it is an experience that is being bought, and to some extent everyone's experience will be different depending on their individual tastes and preferences. Even where people are not spending a great deal of money (such as in a leisure centre or cinema), their enjoyment of the experience cannot be guaranteed.

Trust

The three most expensive purchases that most people make are:

1 A house
2 A car
3 A holiday

While the first two are tangible products that you can see, touch and compare, the third cannot be experienced until it has been bought. It is therefore vital that you have confidence in who is providing you with the holiday or who recommended it to you. In any leisure and tourism setting, customers need to feel they can trust the advice given by staff and, indeed, trust them with their health and safety. This is an important element of customer service.

Enjoyment is hard to quantify

'You can't please everyone' is a phrase that is true of leisure and tourism organisations. Scandinavian Seaways have the occasional complaint that the food on the ship is not 'English'; the food does tend to be Scandinavian but there is always a large choice. Some people very rarely describe anything as excellent or great, whereas others enthuse about many things that they experience. It is therefore very difficult to quantify people's enjoyment and very often it is only unsatisfactory comments that can be recorded.

Varying levels of customer expectation and satisfaction

Welcome on board

Sailing is the only form of travel that is balm to the soul. When you are sailing, you have time. Time to relax, time to enjoy a good meal in one of our restaurants and time to enjoy yourself and each other's company.

I am proud to be able to say that SCAN-DINAVIAN SEAWAYS' ships offer a unique experience to our guests. No effort has been spared to provide a wealth of first-class opportunities for you to enjoy your time on board. Bon voyage!

Bo-Lennart Thorbjörnsson, Group Director, SCANDINAVIAN SEAWAYS, Kopenhagen

Customers have a variety of expectations. On a Scandinavian Seaways crossing some customers want to have a quiet crossing, spending most of their time resting in their cabin. Others wish to enjoy an active crossing with entertainment. A variety of activities are offered for the customers to enjoy if they so choose, and therefore the different customer expectations of the crossing can be satisfied. Customers are satisfied when their expectations are met, and Scandinavian Seaways seek to exceed customer expectations.

The salesperson as part of the service

One of the main differences between selling a physical product such as a computer and selling a leisure and tourism product is that in leisure and tourism, the salesperson may often be part of the product. For example you may be selling a set of dance lessons where you will be the instructor; it is therefore important that you appear to the customers as someone who looks appropriate for that role.

The customer as part of the service

Leisure and tourism activities are usually only as good as the customer is prepared to make them. Other customers can also affect the enjoyment that individuals gain from an activity.

Services cannot be stored

Any chocolate that is not sold today can be sold tomorrow, but a theatre seat that is not sold for today's performance cannot be sold tomorrow. Even if the play is repeated, it will be a separate performance and the opportunity of selling the seat for today's performance will have been lost.

CASE STUDY: CUSTOMER SERVICE IN DFDS SCANDINAVIAN SEAWAYS

DFDS A/S is an important Danish shipping company operating a fleet of ships in the North Sea under the **brand name** Scandinavian Seaways (see Figure 2.4). These ships operate out of the UK on long sea crossings as follows (see Figure 2.5):

Harwich (UK) → Hamburg (Germany)
Harwich (UK) → Esbjerg (Denmark)
Harwich (UK) → Gothenburg (Sweden)
Newcastle (UK) → Gothenburg (Sweden)
Newcastle (UK) → Ijmuiden near
                  Amsterdam (Netherlands)

Scandinavian Seaways Limited is the part of the business responsible for selling Scandinavian Seaways products in the UK. These products include sea crossings and holiday packages as well.

Scandinavian Seaways products involve long sea crossings (Harwich–Hamburg takes 20 hours; Harwich–Gothenburg takes 24

FIGURE 2.4 *MS Princess of Scandinavia*

hours) and so they are not competing in precisely the same market as the channel tunnel and short Dover–Calais sea crossings. They cannot transport you to your destination quickly and so they must find a different **competitive advantage** i.e. something to make you book with them rather than taking a short sea crossing and a long drive or flying. Their **unique selling point** is the quality of the onboard experience. Brochure prices seem very expensive when compared with short sea crossings, but Scandinavian Seaways services continue to be heavily booked because the real price competition is not with the short sea crossings, but with the price of air travel or a short sea crossing plus at least two nights quality hotel accommodation.

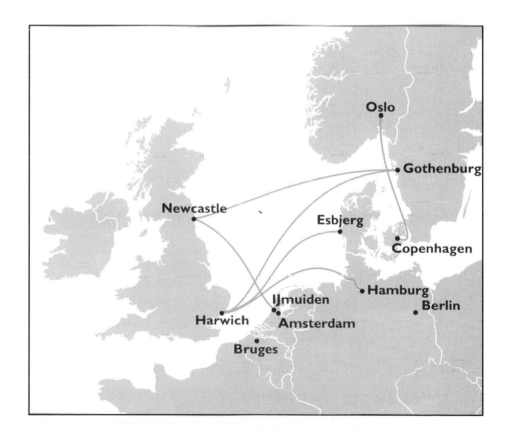

FIGURE 2.5 *Route map*

Amenities
To us, you are more than a passenger – you are our guest. Whatever your destination, your holiday begins the moment you step on board.

A wonderful choice of restaurants and bars. Whether you are looking for fine dining or a great value family supper, your *TravelLiner* will offer the best of every world.

There's never a dull moment on board – you can simply relax on the sun decks or in one of the lounges or watch the latest film in the cinema, dance the night away at the disco, enjoy the live entertainment in the lounge, relax in the sauna, try your luck at the casino, take advantage of the tax free shopping or on some ships take a dip in the swimming pool and pamper yourself in the solarium.

Source: Scandinavian Seaways brochure

In 1994, IPC Magazines conducted a holiday survey to discover how satisfied magazine readers were with various tour operators. As you can see, Scandinavian Seaways customers were most likely to reuse the company (see Figure 2.6).

Scandinavian Seaways see sales as an integral part of customer service, according to

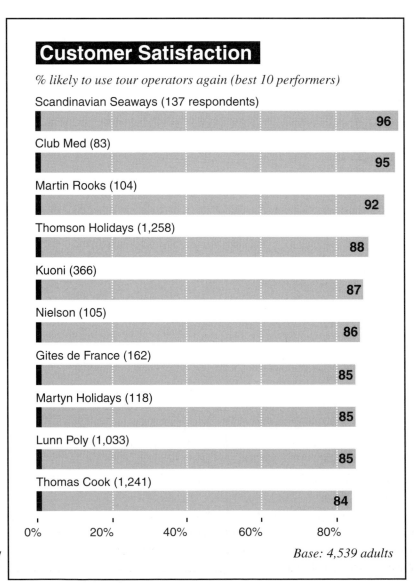

Customer Satisfaction

% likely to use tour operators again (best 10 performers)

Scandinavian Seaways (137 respondents) — 96

Club Med (83) — 95

Martin Rooks (104) — 92

Thomson Holidays (1,258) — 88

Kuoni (366) — 87

Nielson (105) — 86

Gites de France (162) — 85

Martyn Holidays (118) — 85

Lunn Poly (1,033) — 85

Thomas Cook (1,241) — 84

0%   20%   40%   60%   80%

FIGURE 2.6 *IPC Magazines Holiday Survey 1994*

Base: 4,539 adults

INVESTIGATING SALES AND SELLING AS PART OF CUSTOMER SERVICE

Hamish Gibson (customer sales and service manager). The customer service begins when people phone to make an initial enquiry or make a booking – on average calls are answered in five seconds, but this will vary depending on the time of year and the time of day. The aim is that 90 per cent of calls should be answered within 15 seconds. In order to achieve this, it is important that the telesales staff are efficient at dealing with customer enquiries. The target is that calls should be dealt with within 225 seconds so that the telesales operator can be free to deal with the next call. On one day in August 1996, the average call length was 219 seconds, with 1,211 incoming calls of which 28 (2.3 per cent) were not answered because the customer hung up. While staff hope that these people will call back later, there is always the possibility that these unanswered calls represent lost business.

Targets have been set for:

- Call duration (225 seconds)
- Conversion rate (i.e. the number of sales that result from calls – usually one sale is made from every 4.3 calls received)
- The number of travel insurances sold (commission is received by the company for the sale of travel insurance and this is an important source of income as well as providing the customer with 'care')
- The amount of time staff are on the phone, or inactive (if staff are always on the phone leaving other calls unanswered, there may be a need to employ more staff or train existing staff better. On the other hand if staff are unoccupied for significant periods there may be overstaffing).

Telesales staff receive training before they are allowed to speak to customers, and this lasts from three weeks to six months depending on the learning ability of the staff and the complexity of the products with which they will be dealing. Their role is vital as they are the customer's first point of contact with the company. In that training, they are given product knowledge and they are sent by the company during the course of their employment to experience destinations so that they can give advice to customers based on personal experience. They are taught to listen to the customer and help the customer to focus on what is *really* wanted. Often they will only have a vague idea (such as a short break somewhere or a holiday in Sweden), and it is up to the telesales staff to help the customer to decide by asking questions about their budget and their preferences. Staff are taught to listen for key words such as a date that is mentioned by the customer which may be very important in determining price.

Staff are trained to build a rapport quickly with the customers by the giving of names and asking the customer for their name. If the customer replies 'Mr Jones' then the salesperson will call the customer by that name, and if the customer replies 'Louise', then first names will be used. Names are used a lot in the conversation, as are key phrases such as 'have you considered?' If the particular product that the customer is enquiring about is fully booked already, it is important to add to that information – 'however what I can offer you is . . .'. Similarly, information on price is referred to as a 'price sandwich' i.e. the price will be accompanied by a reminder of just what is included for a figure that sounds very expensive.

At the end of every call which has resulted in a booking, the details are always read back to the customer so that no misunderstandings can arise and the customer knows what to expect. However, you will remember from the mission statement that it is the aim of the company to exceed these expectations, using the phrase 'to deliver a level of service to both delight and surprise our customers'.

Scandinavian Seaways attach a great deal of importance to customer feedback. This feedback can take a number of forms, notably:

- Letters of complaint
- Phone calls
- On-board surveys
- Port surveys

Letters of complaint usually deal with specific one-off incidents, but each complaint is carefully logged on a database by Kerry Oxley, the customer care supervisor, who can check for patterns which may reveal part of the ser-

FIGURE 2.7 *Scandinavian Seaways customer sales and service personnel*

vice that is failing to deliver consistently good customer service.

Spontaneous feedback from customers is likely to over-emphasise complaints, and so more proactive methods of research are undertaken. One of these methods is that Scandinavian Seaways managers regularly phone a small sample of recent passengers and ask them how much they enjoyed the product. Additionally Hamish Gibson (customer sales and service manager) regularly goes to the quayside with a clipboard and conducts a survey of passengers who have just checked in, and are about to board the ship, to gain feedback on the booking operation. Finally, on board the ship comment cards are available in English and German, however you will notice that compared with those used by other organisations, these are very unstructured (see Figure 2.8).

As a result of customer feedback, a telephone information system has been established which provides recorded information advising customers, their friends and rela-

tions whether ships are running to time or if any delays have occurred.

MS Hamburg (see Figure 2.9) Programme
4.30 pm departure
5.00–5.30 pm Table reservations taken by the headwaiter in the Alster Restaurant or Four Seasons Restaurant, deck 6 (please specify smoking or non-smoking)
6.00 pm Horse-racing in the Mayfair Lounge, deck 6
10.00 pm Showtime. 'Hamburg hour' in the Mayfair Lounge, deck 6
8.00–11.00 am Breakfast Buffet in the Alster Restaurant and Four Seasons Restaurant, deck 6
8.00 am until arrival: A simple breakfast is served in the Coffee Shop, deck 6
10.30 am: Pirate Club for children, Mayfair Lounge, deck 6
11.15 am: Bingo, Mayfair Lounge
1.00 pm: Arrival

Comments

We in Scandinavian Seaways want very much to offer our customers products and services of the highest possible standard.

To further this objective, if there are areas in which you feel there is room for improvement we would very much like to hear from you.

If you are satisfied with what you have experienced on board, we hope you will tell your family and friends about your trip.

Yours sincerely,
The Crew

Comments:

Name (if convenient):

Cabin no: Date:

Ship:

SCANDINAVIAN SEAWAYS
A BETTER WAY OF TRAVELLING

FIGURE 2.8 *Comment card*

Once on board, customers receive a 12 page glossy brochure giving them information on ship board facilities and events.

Scandinavian Seaways have a number of internal customers. The ships themselves are a customer of Scandinavian Seaways Ltd as they need the UK sales operation to give them their passengers. Scandinavian Seaways rely on hotels and self-catering cottage agencies to supply them with accommodation and

they can present a particular problem – if they provide unsatisfactory service (such as a hotel failing to deliver the standard of accommodation promised) it is Scandinavian Seaways who the customer will blame.

One way in which Scandinavian Seaways ensures good customer service is through communication between internal customers. There are monthly meetings onboard each of the ships where the customer sales and service manager, the group travel manager, the marketing manager, the customer care supervisor and the passenger manager meet with the ship's chief purser, other of the ship's department heads and usually the ship's captain. At these meetings, customer service issues are discussed and the practicality of any initiatives that either the ship staff or the shore staff wish to introduce.

One example of good communication between internal customers occurred when I visited the port. Many customers arrive by the boat train (a special train from London to the port direct), but on this occasion, the train operator (an internal customer) cancelled the boat train, leaving the passengers to travel to the port by a slow train that didn't arrive until 3.20 pm. Passengers should have boarded at 2.30 pm so that the ship was ready to sail at 3.30 pm. The passenger manager had to negotiate with the ship's captain for the MS Hamburg to delay its departure for half an hour with the possibility that all the passengers would be late arriving in Germany.

Even in a business that devotes as much attention to customer service as Scandinavian Seaways, complaints do still occur and these are all dealt with by Kerry Oxley (customer care supervisor). All complaints are logged on arrival on a computerised database, and an acknowledgment letter is normally sent out within two days. Sometimes the complaint will be dealt with by a standard letter but most complaints need investigation as they involve a service provided by an internal customer. The investigation is carried out by a ship board meeting or by sending a fax to the service provider such as an agency sup-

FIGURE 2.9 *MS Hamburg*

plying Danish country cottages, asking specific questions, but the response can sometimes be evasive in which case further questions need to be asked. The point is that the speed of the final response is determined by the provider of the specific service about which the complaint was made.

Scandinavian Seaways are anxious to ensure that the service provider pays for any compensation due to the customer. If the customer's complaint is justified, then they can be compensated by a part-refund to reflect any extra expense to the customer (such as additional hotel costs), or a discount on the price of future travel. In cases where service has been unsatisfactory, customers are asked to make future bookings through a special administration desk which is staffed by the most experienced staff. The pattern for dealing with complaints is always:

> receive → log → acknowledge → ---
> investigate → reply

The complaints database is regularly analysed to look for patterns in complaints to see if, in any area of the operation, customer service is failing to be consistent.

Key Skills Hint: Communication using images

When making a presentation, be sure to avoid just talking at your audience by using images such as photographs, slides or overhead projector transparencies to illustrate what you have to say.

TASK 3

Use the information in this section, plus your own research, to word process a report of 1,000 words outlining the sales and selling aspect of customer service in leisure and tourism. The report should:

- Explain the functions and objectives of selling
- Describe sales techniques
- Explain the duties, responsibilities and necessary qualities of sales staff in leisure and tourism organisations
- Explain the value of sales administration systems
- Explain what makes the selling of leisure and tourism products/services different

CHECKLIST OF PORTFOLIO EVIDENCE

☑ report

TASK 4

Select either Scandinavian Seaways or another leisure and tourism organisation to investigate. Prepare and present a presentation to the rest of your group which should last up to ten minutes and which is supported with aids such as illustrations, tables, charts etc. The presentation should look at the following areas in your chosen organisation:

- Functions and objectives of selling as part of customer service
- Techniques used in selling
- Staff duties and responsibilities in selling
- Staff qualities needed for selling
- The value of the sales administration systems used

CHECKLIST OF PORTFOLIO EVIDENCE

☑ tutor's comments on your presentation

3

Analysing customer service quality

....

K e y   A i m s

This section will enable you to:

- explain how organisations assess the quality of their customer service
- appraise customer service quality criteria
- make judgements about the quality of customer service
- suggest how customer service could be improved in chosen organisations

Before analysing customer service quality it is worth referring back to section 1, to reconsider some components of customer service: caring for customers (external and internal), meeting customer needs, achieving customer satisfaction, meeting customer expectations, maintaining security and safety.

ASSESSING THE QUALITY OF CUSTOMER SERVICE

The quality of customer service in an organisation is complex. It is made up of a variety of **criteria** which can measure the quality of the service that is provided to customers. The main thirteen are as follows:

- Reliability of service
- Consistency
- Health and safety
- Accessibility
- Availability
- Timing
- Price
- Value for money
- Staffing levels
- Quality of staff
- Enjoyment of experience
- Provision for individual needs
- Service levels

Have you ever completed one of these (see Figure 3.1)?

McDonald's

RESTAURANT REVIEW

"McDonald's is committed to providing hot fresh food with fast efficient friendly service in clean and pleasant surroundings"

Please take a minute to review our restaurant and tell us how we measure up to the above statement. When you've completed this form place it in the suggestion box. Thanks for helping us to serve you better.

PLEASE TICK	VERY GOOD	GOOD	FAIR	POOR	VERY POOR
SERVICE	☺	☺	😐	☹	☹
FOOD	☺	☺	😐	☹	☹
COURTESY	☺	☺	😐	☹	☹
CLEANLINESS	☺	☺	😐	☹	☹
VALUE FOR MONEY	☺	☺	😐	☹	☹

DATE OF VISIT ____________ TIME OF VISIT ____________

COMMENTS

How can we serve you better? ____________

What would make you return more frequently? ____________

What facilities does this McDonald's lack that you would like to see added? ____________

Please write here any good comments or suggestions you may have (especially if you feel strongly about any of the above). ____________

How often do you visit our Restaurants?
Daily ☐
Weekly ☐
Monthly ☐
Infrequently ☐

Please tick
Male ☐
Female ☐
Age Group
12-15 ☐
16-24 ☐
25-34 ☐
35+ ☐

Please speak to the Restaurant Manager if you wish to discuss your comments further or alternatively you can call: Customer Services on 0181 444 4343

FIGURE 3.1 *McDonald's customer comment card*

Reliability and consistency

Reliability is an important criteria for judging quality of customer service: if a service is excellent but cannot be relied upon, customers will not return.

Consistency is very similar to reliability, as it is a way of measuring whether the customer always receives the same level of service. The subtle difference is, if you expect a train service to be reliable you expect the trains to depart and arrive according to the published timetable, but if you expect it to be consistent, then you would expect the same level of friendly service from the on-board buffet on Wednesday as you received from different staff on Tuesday.

Health and safety

Most health and safety standards are set by laws. Therefore failure to comply cannot only lose customers but put employees of an organisation in court. It is important to observe procedures rigorously. In that way, if anything does go wrong the organisation is protected. For example in a case of food poisoning, 'A person accused of an offence under the Food Safety Act 1990 may plead that he had taken *all reasonable precautions* and

On Saturday 6 July, Colchester Salvation Army band had an engagement to play on the bandstand in the centre of Ostend at 3 pm. The band left Colchester ahead of schedule at 8.25 am and they arrived at the Channel Tunnel still well ahead of schedule at 10.15 am. The bandmaster had calculated that the journey from Calais to Ostend should take around 75 minutes, so if they went through the tunnel by 11.20 am, they would be away from Calais by 1 o'clock European time and have plenty of time to arrive, unload the coach and relax before giving their concert.

The tension started to build when it was announced that a train had broken down in the tunnel, and that there were other trains behind that would have to reverse out before the faulty train could be recovered. The band actually arrived at Ostend at 2.45 pm and the concert began only two minutes late, but the Tunnel's competitive advantage of speed had been let down by poor reliability.

exercised *all due diligence* to avoid the offence being committed by himself or by someone under his control' (my italics) (Donaldson, RJ, *Essential Food Hygiene*, Royal Society of Health, London, 1993).

Accessibility

Is the leisure and tourism facility accessible to people who might want to use it? For example, does it have wheelchair access, or (if on several floors), is there a lift?

Availability and timing

Is the leisure and tourism facility available to people who might want to use it at appropriate times? A restaurant that only opens from 10 am–12 am and 2 pm–5 pm is likely to lose customers.

Price and value for money

Prices are a very important criteria for judging the quality of customer service. If a customer feels that an attraction was 'not worth the money', it is because they have not achieved the same level of satisfaction as they received for spending the same amount of money on something else.

If something is good value for money it does not mean that it is necessarily inexpensive. A customer may feel that £10 for a day in a theme park was good value for money, whereas £1 for entry to a poor quality exhibition may be considered 'a rip-off'. For example, a brochure of 'value for money breaks' called *Superbreaks* contains a stay in the Brighton Grand Hotel for two people sharing a double room in the spring, priced at £140 for one night, bed and breakfast, while on the same page in the brochure, one night's stay for two people sharing a double room at the Royal Albion Hotel is priced at £70.

Staffing levels

Leisure and tourism organisations are known as **labour intensive**; this means that the cost of staff makes up the largest part of their costs. The main reason that some hotels are much more expensive than others is often not because one offers more facilities than another, but rather because the more expensive hotel employs more staff so that customers can receive a better service.

A characteristic of Forte Travel Lodge and similar hotels where you pay a fixed price for the room, is that very few staff are employed. There is no reception staffed 24 hours, no restaurant, no bar. You get what you pay for, a clean and comfortable room with a kettle, a television and a bathroom. This has become increasingly popular:

'What actually happened was that 134 hotels closed down, while 102 new hotels opened which were better suited to what 1990s travellers are seeking. It is the old, small hotels in towns that are closing, while roadside lodges such as Forte's Travel Lodge that are the popular alternative. According to *The Guardian*, ''They have established brand credibility. People know what they will be getting and how much they will have to pay'' '. (Lyons, AJ, *Essential Economics* Hodder & Stoughton, London, 1996)

In many leisure and tourism organisations, minimum staffing levels are dictated by health and safety regulations.

Quality of staff

When assessing the quality of staff, it is the minimum level of quality that must be measured. For example, if your very efficient receptionist is off sick, and you have had to employ a temp who knows very little about the organisation, the fact that he or she is a temp will be irrelevant to the customer who will still expect the same level of customer service.

All members of staff have off-days when they find it difficult to be constantly cheerful (for example they may be feeling unwell). Therefore 'always cheerful' might be an expectation of your staff but it may not be an appropriate quality criteria for staff. On the other hand, even on an off-day staff can be expected to be polite, smart and knowledgeable, therefore these might be appropriate criteria against which to assess your staff.

Enjoyment of experience

It may be impossible to guarantee that every customer will enjoy the experience of visiting your leisure and tourism organisation: often it can be affected by things over which you have no control, for example the weather may be bad or the customer may have a quarrel with his companions. However, thought should always be given to how you can do your best to ensure that the customer's potential for enjoyment is maximised. For example a canal tour operator in the Belgian city of Bruges (see Figure 3.2) may be faced with a group, with one boat already half full. In a situation like this it would be best to avoid splitting up the group (and certainly avoid

FIGURE 3.2 *A canal boat tour of Bruges (Belgium)*

insisting that a couple are split between two boats).

Provision for individual needs

The only way to ensure that individual needs are met is to build in flexibility. Some years ago the main hamburger chain in Britain was Wimpy which gave a choice between a burger with or without fried onions. During the 1980s hamburgers became much more sophisticated with the arrival of American chains who produced large numbers of burgers ready and waiting to be served, complete with various relishes, garnishes and ketchup. If you wanted a burger without these additions your wish could often not be accommodated. In the 1990s the emphasis is much more on the individual customer than standardisation of the product, and so if you ask for a plain hamburger with cheese and no relish you will be told 'Certainly sir. That will take about four minutes, so if you would like to take a seat, I will bring it over when its ready'.

Service levels

Airlines offer various levels of service and while most passengers travel 'Economy' class, some opt for the extra expense and service level offered by 'Club' or 'First' class. These classes essentially provide the same service i.e. air travel from point A to point B at a particular time, but some people are willing to pay double for the extra service provided in club class, where the food is better and the seating less crowded.

APPRAISING CUSTOMER SERVICE

Like assessing, appraising is another measuring word. In this element it means putting the various quality criteria covered earlier into an order of importance. This will of course vary from customer to customer and, much more so, from activity to activity.

Commodore and Commodore De Luxe Cabins

If you require a little more luxury and special attention you can choose our Commodore or Commodore De Luxe cabins. These normally have two single beds, have a sea view and are equipped with all the facilities you would expect – such as lounge area†, writing desk, minibar, hair dryer, radio, TV*, complimentary stationery, bath and hand towels, shampoo, soap, sewing kit, body lotion, nail file, shoe polish sponge and a newspaper from the port of departure. Priority boarding, room service, table reservation facilities and breakfast in your cabin is also included in the fare.

*TV available on Copenhagen-Oslo routes only
†Lounge area in Commodore De Luxe cabins only.

FIGURE 3.3 *Scandinavian Seways Commodore class*

ANALYSING THE QUALITY OF CUSTOMER SERVICE

While a good leisure and tourism organisation will aim to meet the expectations of its customers, an excellent organisation will aim to exceed those expectations. The problem for large organisations is that although they may have first class training programmes and policy documents for customer service, it is difficult to know exactly what is happening on the ground.

Feedback from customers

It is important for businesses to receive feedback from their customers: if the business is doing things that customers like, then this fact should be publicised; if things are going wrong, it is important that the management are made aware that the actual level of service does not relate to the quality criteria or to customer expectations. British customers have a reputation for 'not complaining' but this does not necessarily mean that they are easily satisfied – they are likely to say nothing about unsatisfactory service but never return. Even if customers are asked to give feedback it is difficult to persuade them to give honest feedback face-to-face. For this reason many leisure and tourism organisations provide their customers with feedback forms which are designed to be simple and quick to complete as in Figure 3.1. Even when the response card is made simple and quick to complete, many customers will not wish to make the effort to respond. Therefore some businesses give their customers an incentive to complete the questionnaire (see Figure 3.4).

Positive feedback can be very motivating for staff – it is good to know that your customers think you are doing a good job. Without this actively solicited feedback, only complaints are likely to come through, and the 99 per cent of satisfied customers will never be heard. Not only do customers feel valued by the active seeking of their opinions, but staff can gain satisfaction as well.

Where common areas of concern can be seen in several responses, these can then be addressed. It is therefore an efficient way for the business to operate as not only are the customers' views learned quickly, but also cheaply, without the need to hire people to conduct extra research. This is turn leads the organisation to become more effective, as the operations can be tailored to respond to the wishes of customers as expressed in their feedback. Cases of serious disappointment can be followed up with a special offer to the dissatisfied customer.

Rather than relying entirely on customer feedback, other methods can be devised: the use of 'company spies' or 'the mystery customer' is a widely used technique. This is when a market researcher visits an organisation, and reports back to the management on just how well their quality criteria are operating on the ground. Often the individual who gives less than satisfactory customer service is named in the report, possibly damaging his or her career prospects. It is therefore sensible to assume that any customer could be a company spy and so ensure that excellent customer service is delivered to each customer. However, although company spies or mystery customers are a useful way of improving standards as they keep management informed of what is really happening, they can lead to mistrust between staff and management. Poor relations between management and staff creates an unpleasant atmosphere which is bad for customer service.

ANALYSING THE QUALITY OFFERED IN RELATED MARKETS

Related markets are those which may affect the customers' view of your organisation. As such, it is not just direct competitors that provide impressions.

- *Direct competition:* if there are two cinemas in one town then they are obviously in direct competition; if one offers better customer service than the other then it has a competitive advantage

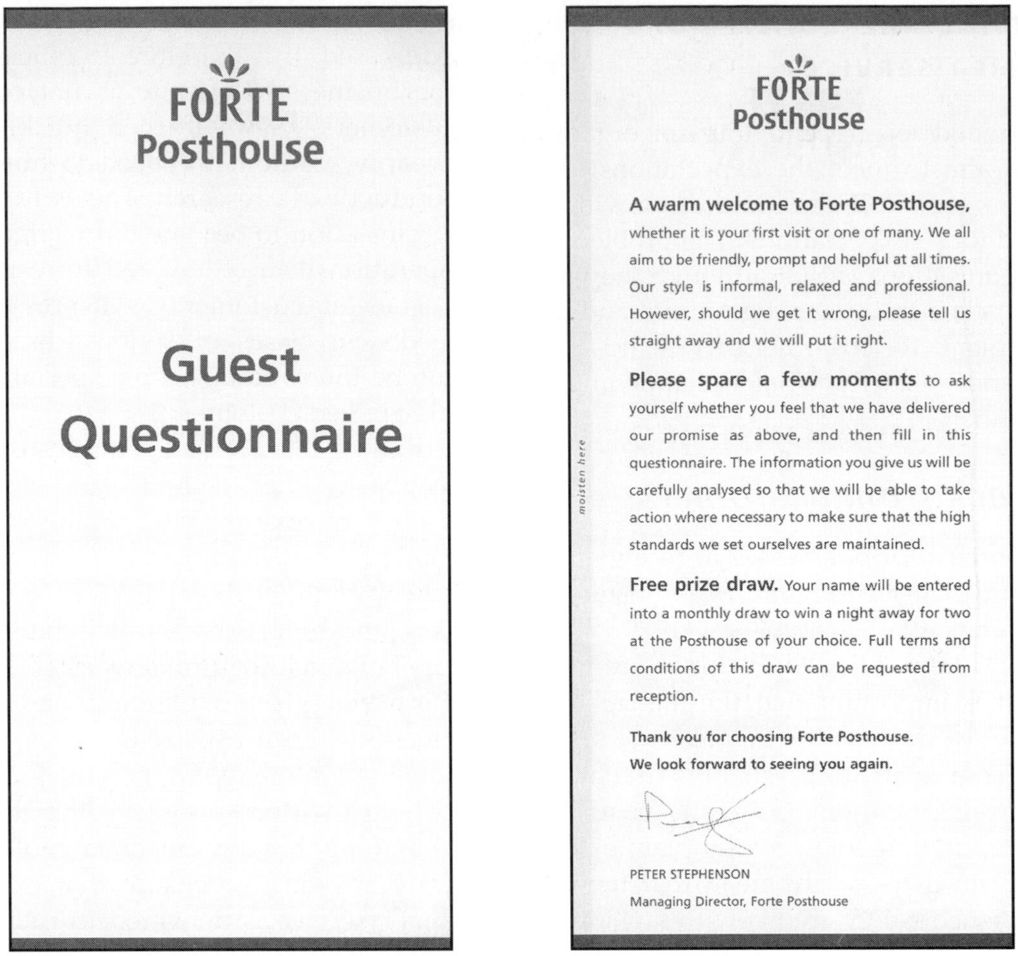
FORTE
Posthouse

Guest
Questionnaire

FORTE
Posthouse

moisten here

A warm welcome to Forte Posthouse, whether it is your first visit or one of many. We all aim to be friendly, prompt and helpful at all times. Our style is informal, relaxed and professional. However, should we get it wrong, please tell us straight away and we will put it right.

Please spare a few moments to ask yourself whether you feel that we have delivered our promise as above, and then fill in this questionnaire. The information you give us will be carefully analysed so that we will be able to take action where necessary to make sure that the high standards we set ourselves are maintained.

Free prize draw. Your name will be entered into a monthly draw to win a night away for two at the Posthouse of your choice. Full terms and conditions of this draw can be requested from reception.

Thank you for choosing Forte Posthouse.
We look forward to seeing you again.

PETER STEPHENSON
Managing Director, Forte Posthouse

FIGURE 3.4 *Forte Posthouse guest questionnaire*

- *Other organisations in the same business:* while a fish and chip shop is not in direct competition with a Chinese take-away, if one offers a faster service than the other, this will affect customers' expectations as both are in the take-away food business
- *Related service organisations:* a theatre could be related to a cinema in terms of its foyer services (such as the provision of refreshments). One might expect similar standards in each
- *Unrelated service organisations:* organisations outside the leisure and tourism industry may affect customer expectations. For example, supermarkets have introduced policies to keep queues to a minimum at checkout tills. This is achieved by keeping staff, in other parts of the store, on standby to assist, and may affect customers' expectations of a reasonable time delay in purchasing a ticket.

COMPARING CUSTOMER SERVICE

Benchmarking is a term used to describe the process of measuring an organisation's performance against that of other organisations. Internal benchmarking compares performance between different parts of the same organisation, while external benchmarking can make comparisons with quite different types of organisations. For example is your hotel foyer as bright and welcoming as that in the offices next door?

MAKING RECOMMENDATIONS FOR IMPROVEMENTS

This element has dealt with the key customer service criteria. When making recommenda-tions for improvement in any particular organisation, you should: appraise and ana-lyse the quality of customer service in the organisation, analyse the quality of customer service in related markets, and compare the organisation you are examining to the others you have looked at; then you can make your recommendations.

TASK 5

Make notes on how each of the thir-teen quality criteria listed on page 36 can be assessed by leisure and tourism organisations.

CHECKLIST OF PORTFOLIO EVIDENCE

☑ set of notes

TASK 6

You have been asked to plan and then deliver a presentation based on an in-depth analysis of customer service in one leisure and tourism organisation of your choice (probably one well known to you). Your presentation must cover the following:

- How do the quality criteria listed on page 36 apply to the chosen organisation?
- Which are the most important, and which the least important in this organisation?
- To what extent does customer ser-vice in the organisation meet these criteria? Try to seek the views of other customers. You may also act as a 'mystery customer' yourself.
- An analysis of customer service in at least one organisation in a related market, such as a direct competitor. Once again you may need to act as a 'mystery customer'.
- Compare customer service in the organisations you have looked at, and on the basis of your findings, make recommendations for improvements to customer service in the organisation you chose to look at.

CHECKLIST OF PORTFOLIO EVIDENCE

☑ tutor's comments on your planning of your presentation
☑ tutor's comments on your delivery of your presentation

SECTION

Review of the Unit

The final section of the customer service unit is an action unit. In other words you have to put into practice what you have learned from the first three sections. You must take part in both the delivery and the **evaluation** of customer service.

Figure 4.1 is provided on page 46 for you to record details about your own customer service. You will need a separate copy for each of the three customer service situations you submit for your portfolio. The customer

service situations may be ones that arise naturally from a work experience placement or a part-time job. However, if you are not employed in a leisure and tourism situation, you will need to set up a simulation. In either case, the customer service situation you are dealing with should ideally be videoed. If this is not practical, then witness statements from your workplace supervisor or your tutor must be submitted.

TASK 7

Provide customer service for three different customers in different situations. For each situation you must:

- Identify the objective or objectives of the service delivery (i.e. what are you trying to achieve?).
- Prioritise customer needs and identify the service quality criteria that the customer will be judging.
- Use appropriate communication methods to satisfy the needs of the customer and achieve the objectives that you described.

- Record any customer information that is necessary.

Your handling of each situation must be recorded, preferably by video but if this is not possible then by the witness statement of your supervisor or tutor.

CHECKLIST OF PORTFOLIO EVIDENCE

☑ video or witness statement describing your provision of customer service

TASK 8

Evaluate your performance in each of the three customer service situations carried out in Task 7. You should judge your performance against the objectives that you identified and against the quality criteria expected by the customer. Your evaluation should include feedback from the rest of your group, or work colleagues; and from your supervisor or tutor. Record all this on Figure 4.2 provided on page 47.

CHECKLIST OF PORTFOLIO EVIDENCE

☑ evaluation of your own performance
☑ feedback from other members of your group

TASK 9

Using the record sheets as your starting point, produce a report making recommendations on how you could improve the customer service that you have provided. Identify training needs for staff and any improvements that could be made by the organisation.

CHECKLIST OF PORTFOLIO EVIDENCE

☑ record sheets
☑ report

Assignment checklist

For each situation, consider the following:

What types of customer am I dealing with?

- Internal or external
- Age group
- Cultural background
- Customers with specific needs
- Individuals or groups

What is the nature of the customer service situation?

- Customer requiring information
- Customer requiring help with a problem
- Customer with a complaint
- Customer needing sales advice

What are the priorities for this customer?

- Reliability or consistency
- Health and safety
- Accessibility and availability
- Price
- Value for money
- Staffing levels and quality of staff
- Timing of service
- Enjoyment of experience
- Provision for individual needs
- Service levels

What is the best way to communicate in this situation?

- Good personal image
- Verbal
- Non-verbal
- Telephone
- Written
- Feedback loop

How will I best record customer information?

- Booking form
- Order form
- Register
- Statement of account or bill
- Issuing of a ticket
- Memo
- Email

FIGURE 4.1 *Assignment checklist*

Describe the customer service situation and identify the type of customer	Describe the needs of this customer and the customer service criteria to be judged	Describe the communication methods that you have used and how this is recorded	Note necessary customer information and where and
Briefly describe the objectives of your customer service	Your own evaluation of your performance	Your colleagues'/group members evaluation of your performance	Supervisor or tutor's evaluation of your performance Supervisor/ Tutor signature _____ Date:...............

FIGURE 4.2 *Developing customer service in leisure and tourism*

Glossary

analyse: to carry out a detailed examination.

brand: a brand is the name given by a business to one or a number of its products. It could be the producer's own name or it could be something that describes what you are likely to find, e.g. Holiday Inn Garden Court.

brand name: a named product that the consumer believes to be different from similar products.

brand recognition: customers will instantly recognise a successful brand and will know what to expect from it. For example, most people know that a 'Mars' is a chocolate bar.

competitive advantage: something that makes your product stand out as being better or more attractive than similar products.

costs: the amount of money that a business has to spend in order to produce its products.

criteria: the standards by which something is judged. (Note that criteria is a plural word, if there is only one then it is a criterion).

customer interface: any place where customers are served in any way by a business.

evaluate: to weigh up (in this case how good something is) on the basis of available evidence.

evaluation: the writing up of your findings when you have weighed up (in this case how good something is) on the basis of available evidence.

franchises: a franchise is when a business develops a well known brand, and allows other businesses to use that brand in exchange for payment. The franchisee has to agree to maintain the standards that are associated with that brand.

front of house: staff who have direct contact with customers such as receptionists.

internal customer: departments within your business or other businesses that you depend on to help you deliver good service to your customers.

labour intensive: a business where a lot of labour is used to deliver a product as opposed to machines. Whilst cars can be built by robots, meals cannot yet be served by machines.

locally: on package holidays, some excursions can be booked when you book the holiday. However, a number of excursions are provided by coach businesses located in the resort and the holiday representative will receive payment for selling these excursions.

private sector: any business not owned by the

government in any form. Private sector businesses include 'Public Companies' which are owned by members of the public of the public who are shareholders.

public sector: any business owned by central or local government.

revenue: the income that a business receives from sales.

segment of the market (or market segment): part of the market that can be targeted because it contains customers with similar wants, desires or expectations.

subsidiary: a business that is part of a larger business (for example Forte Posthouse is part of the Granada group of companies).

unique selling point: something that makes your product special and no one else supplies.

CROSSWORD: INVESTIGATING CUSTOMER SERVICE

ACROSS

2 Your ability to do the job
5 When customers come back
6 Offering something that your competitors do not
7 A formal way of ensuring that information gets to the person who will act on it
8 The customer's first impression of you can be based on this
9 What customers are led to believe they will receive

DOWN

1 How well you do your job
3 The public's view of your organisation
4 Staff who regularly deal directly with the public

See foot of page for answers.

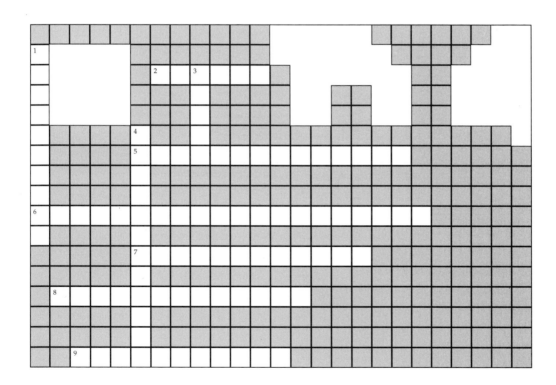

Index

Aachen   14–15
Alsace   14

backroom staff   1
benchmarking   43–4
brand name   14
brand recognition   16
British Airways (BA)   5, 7
Bruges   40

Channel Tunnel   3, 4, 30, 39
Clutterbuck, David   23
communicating   6–8, 14
  with groups   7
  with individuals   6, 14
competitive advantage   24, 30
complaints   21, 32–3
costs   24
cultural background   13
customer interface   25

direct competition   42

effective   12, 18
efficient   8, 12, 32
expectations   4, 32
eye contact   7, 10

face-to-face meetings   10
family groups   13
feedback loops   11
first impressions   8
Forte Travel Lodge   40
friendliness   viii, 24, 27
front of house   1

gestures   7

Gibson, Hamish   28, 32

Hellbrunn Palace   13
Holiday Inn   14–17, 22, 27

internal customer   12

Islam   13

labour intensive   39
Lakes & Mountains   24
Legoland   27
letters   10, 32
Libs, Patrick   27

Mastercard   27
mission statement   3
motivation   3
mystery customer   42

non-verbal communication   6

Odeon Cinemas   5

P&O Ferries   3
personal image   8
private sector   24
profit   5, 24
public sector   24

Ratner, Gerald   27
related service organisations   43
revenue   24
Royal Society of Health   4, 39

Scandinavian Seaways   3, 8, 24, 26, 27, 28,
  29–35

security and safety   4
segment of the market (or market segment)   12,
   14
selling, functions of   20–2
St. Wolfgang   24
Steigenberger Reservation Service   5
Strasbourg   27
subsidiary   15
Superbreaks   39
support staff   1
Sweden   24

telephone speaking   9

unique selling point   15, 49

value adder   5
verbal communication   11

Warner, David   27
written communication   10

Zemke, Ron   5–6